ENGLISH 19TH-CENTURY PRESS-MOULDED GLASS

ENGLISH 19TH-CENTURY PRESS-MOULDED GLASS

COLIN R. LATTIMORE

BARRIE & JENKINS
COMMUNICA-EUROPA

TO ISOBEL
hesterna manent

© Colin R. Lattimore 1979

First published in 1979 by
Barrie & Jenkins Ltd
24 Highbury Crescent, London N5 1RX

ISBN   0 214 20598 3

Designed by Heather Sherratt

Filmset in 11/13 point Baskerville
Printed and bound in Great Britain
by W & J Mackay Limited, Chatham

CONTENTS

LIST OF ILLUSTRATIONS

ACKNOWLEDGEMENTS

I should like to express my appreciation to the many antique dealers, librarians and museum staff who have made the research for this book such a pleasure. In particular, my thanks go to Mr John Brooks, antique glass dealer, for his initial and sustained encouragement and to Mr Bernard Matthew who took such great pains and interest in photographing items from my collection for the illustrations. Finally, I would like to thank the staff and associates of Barrie and Jenkins for their understanding and help in this, my first publication.

INTRODUCTION

IT IS only in recent years that press-moulded glass has received any attention from collectors. However, as with many other of our more recent antiques, it is now attracting a lot of interest as the price of antiques of earlier years rises to almost astronomical proportions. Already many pieces of pressed glass of the last quarter of the nineteenth century, particularly commemorative items, are fetching as many pounds as they would have shillings ten years ago.

In its Victorian heyday, which is roughly 1870–90, production by the Sowerby glasshouse alone was at the rate of one hundred and fifty tons of finished glass per week, and this was only one of the many glasshouses producing pressed glass up and down the country. In spite of this fantastic output, only a hundred years later pieces are not to be found in abundance. There are various reasons for this: one is that by its very nature and method of production it was cheap and once out of fashion would have been discarded. Those pieces that remained with families for sentimental reasons would not have been highly prized on the death of their second-generation owners. They would probably have been put in the dustbin as unworthy of being sold. Having been produced and bought cheaply and being largely utilitarian in nature, they would have been thrown out once chipped, cracked or damaged beyond useful function.

More recently, however, a great interest has been shown in pressed glass in America, which itself has produced vast quantities in the last hundred and fifty years. There has been a brisk export trade to the United States along with many other British antiques.

Nearly all the pieces of glass mentioned or illustrated in this book would originally have been sold for pence and it is in this light that they must be viewed today – not as great examples of nineteenth-century decorative art, but as products of the Industrial Revolution which enabled many more people to possess glass items made less expensive, if also less fine, by mass-production methods. Designs and shapes were limited by the mouldmaker's art, which accounts for the somewhat mechanical appearance of many of the pieces. In the early days of production pressed glass was to cut crystal what Sheffield plate was to sterling silver, a means of possessing an apparently similar piece at a much lower price. Nevertheless, viewed as a type of folk art many of the pieces have a certain naïve charm, although it has to be admitted that some exhibit the worst aspects of Victorian design – a fault not limited to pressed glass.

The story of pressed glass is in many ways a social history of the nineteenth century, and will appeal to the social historian as well as to the antiquarian and the collector.

C.R.L.
Caxton Court,
Caxton,
Cambridge

1 Illustration from *Curiosities of Glass Making* by Apsley Pellatt, London, 1849, showing an early pressing machine.

CHAPTER 1

ORIGINS AND DEVELOPMENT

THE manufacture of glass articles is a very ancient craft and there are basically three ways in which they can be produced: (1) free-blowing; (2) blow-moulding; and (3) press-moulding. It is with the third process that this book is concerned.

Free-blowing is the traditional method of manufacture. A quantity of molten glass (called at this stage 'metal') is taken on to a blowpipe and shaped by blowing it up like a balloon and working on this sphere with various tools to achieve the required shape. This is an expensive method of production – each item is unique and great artistic and manipulative skill is required. The production rate is necessarily slow.

The second method, blow-moulding, still involves the use of the blowpipe but in this case the glass balloon is blown into a multi-part metal (in the more common sense of the word) mould capable of being dismantled to allow easy extraction of the article. The hot, plastic metal (molten glass) takes on to its outer surface the shape and design, if any, of the inner surface of the mould. The advantages of this method are its speed, uniformity, and the lack of the same degree of artistic skill on the part of the blower as that required for free-blown work. The use of moulds results in standard shapes capable of being reproduced many thousands of times. This, from a manufacturer's point of view, is a good thing.

Press-moulding is in some ways an improvement on the second method. Two moulds are used – an inner and an outer one – and the forming is done, not by the human lungs, but by pressure exerted on the inner mould or plunger by hand through a lever system capable of very much greater pressure than can be achieved by the lungs (see Plate 1). There is an apparent disadvantage in this method, since it would seem to restrict designs to those shapes which are always wider at the top than the bottom, or at least no narrower, so that the plunger can be withdrawn. While this is true of individual pressings the problem can be overcome by pressing items such as decanters, which have narrow necks, in two halves. A bottom half and a top half which if pressed upside-down, will fulfil the requirement of being wider at the top than the bottom. The two outer moulds are hinged together in such a way that, after the plungers have been withdrawn, the top half can be placed on top of the bottom half while the metal is still hot, and the two halves sealed together. Articles produced like this will have a horizontal mould line as well as vertical ones. Another way to press bottle shapes is to do so from the bottom, leaving a flange which can be closed over to seal the bottom while the metal is still hot.

There are a number of ways in which pressed articles can be distinguished from blow-moulded ones:

(1) The nature of the mould lines – both types have mould lines caused by the molten glass bulging into the slight gaps between the various pieces of the mould. In blow-moulded pieces these lines are often scarcely noticeable due to the low pressure applied in manufacture, but in press-moulding they are often extremely prominent because the greater pressure used not only forces the glass into the gaps but also tends to force the mould apart, making the gap even larger if there is any 'play' in the assembly. Although the prominence of these mould lines can be modified by fire polishing later, they nevertheless remain a feature of press-moulded glass.

(2) With the exception of pieces like decanters, no part of the inside of a pressed article can be narrower than the levels below it – otherwise the plunger could not be withdrawn. The article can, however, be worked after pressing and before cooling in order to alter its shape. This accounts for such things as the so-called closed baskets (see Plate 2).

(3) Any impressed design on a pressed piece is very much sharper and crisper compared to blow-moulded pieces simply because of the greater pressure in the former process.

(4) Press-moulded pieces can have designs applied to both inner and outer surfaces, although in practice the designs on the inner surface of deep vessels are restricted to trade marks or registered design numbers. The advantage is seen best on shallow pieces such as plates. With blow-moulded pieces the contours of the inner surface always follow those of the outer surface.

2 Three small baskets showing manipulation of the hot glass after pressing. The centre one shows the appearance straight from the mould. The one on the left bears a Sowerby mark.

A type of press-moulding was known to the ancients, and certainly in England in the eighteenth century it was being used to produce the feet of wineglasses, but it was in America that the process was first adapted to the production of hollow ware in the 1820s. It is not clear which of the American glasshouses was the first to introduce press-moulding, but between 1825 and 1830 no fewer than twelve press-moulding patents were taken out, the last of which was taken out by John McGann of Kensington, Pennsylvania. This relates to manufacturing 'glass bottles, decanters of all kinds and other pressed hollow glassware with necks smaller than the cavity or inside diameter of the vessel' by the method just described. For the first forty years in America the presses were operated by hand, but in 1864 the first patent was taken out for a steam-operated glass press.

In Britain progress was relatively slower. The first attempts at pressing hollow ware took place in the 1830s. The first pressing machine was installed by Benjamin Richardson, manager of T. Hawkes and Co., Birmingham, in 1831. A report of the Excise Commission in 1835 recorded the following conversation between a witness and the Commission:

'Was there not a peculiar type of glass imported from America lately?'

'Yes, it was called pressed or intagliated glass.'

'Does it still come in great quantities?'

'No, we have since manufactured it in this country but it was an American invention.'

One of the main reasons for the slower development in Britain, at least in the early stages, was the presence of a glass tax. In 1745 a tax was imposed, by weight, on glass during manufacture which was to last for exactly a hundred years. By 1800 the tax had risen from 9s 4d to 21s 5½d per hundredweight, although at that time it did not appear to be having any marked effect on the production of glass in quantity. By the 1830s when the press-moulding system was being developed the effect was more noticeable since the pressed glass, being much thicker and therefore heavier, attracted more duty, which cut down the financial advantage gained by speed of production. However in 1845 the tax was finally lifted, with considerable repercussions within the glass industry.

The tax, whose collection had become extremely burdensome, had given rise to backstreet glasshouses producing cheap, illicit goods, the value of which, in London alone, has been estimated at over £65,000 annually. Harry Powell of the Whitefriars Glassworks, writing later in the century, remembered: '. . . the sentry boxes in which the officers of the Excise spent such part of their time in sleeping as was not occupied in harrying the Works manager or being harried by the glasshouse boys'. In order to avoid connivance with the management at least two of these officers were quartered in every glassworks and it was their job to register the total weight of glass used, and not to allow the removal of any finished goods until they too had been weighed. Although the tax was charged on the raw material as it went into the pots, weighing the finished goods was a check that nothing extra had slipped through. The amount of ill-feeling the men caused was brought out in evidence before the Commission of Excise in 1833. It appears that extremely strict control of the works' activities was maintained by the Excise Officers, and failure to comply with their wishes could involve the management in fines of £200–£500 for each offence.

With the lifting of the tax the production of pressed glass began to expand, though only slowly at first, doing little more than copying at much lower cost the fashionable cut glass of the period. Another tax repeal also gave the industry a boost when in 1835 the tax on salt, which had been levied at nine times its retail value, was lifted, giving rise to a large number of cheap pressed-glass salt cellars in pairs, fours and sixes. Many of these, after 1845, were very heavy (see Plate 3).

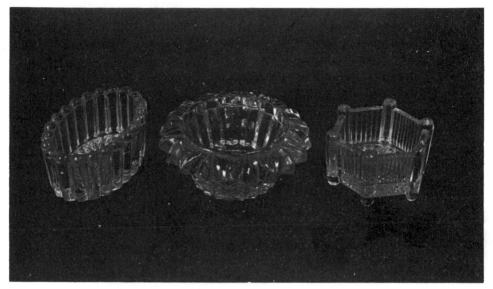

3 Group of salt cellars, c. 1880. *Left to right* Greener, Davidson and Sowerby, each bearing the appropriate trade mark.

Press-moulding was used for four reasons: to give shape to an article; to impress a design or pattern on its surface; to speed up the rate of production; and to reduce the skill necessary in producing the article. The last two have a distinct effect on the ultimate price of the article and help to cut costs considerably if allowed to operate in an unfettered manner. The workmen, however, saw these 'machines' as a potential threat, possibly causing a reduction in their wages and loss of jobs, and a classic industrial wrangle followed which was to last, on and off, for the rest of the century.

The moulds were usually made from cast iron or gunmetal, and were in two or more parts depending on the complexity of the shape. The outer mould could be divided into a base and side-pieces which could consist of up to four parts. The parts were hinged so that the article could be easily removed, and the joints in the mould arranged so that the mould lines on the finished piece would be as inconspicuous as possible. A collar fitted to the top of the mould prevented escape of the glass during pressing and helped to form the lip of the vessel.

The method used was as follows: the basic ingredients (see Chapter 2) were put in a large, hooded fireclay pot or an open pan, depending on whether or not lead was being used in that particular glass mixture. Lead-containing glass was always melted in a hooded pot able to hold many hundredweights of (glass) metal. This was to prevent the gases and possible impurities from the furnace coming into contact with the metal and discolouring it. The pots were housed in a furnace with their openings facing outwards to allow access. Six to twelve pots could be housed in one furnace which, in

4 Engraving of glasshouse furnace, c. 1850, from *Curiosities of Glass Making* by Apsley Pellatt.

Britain in the nineteenth century would have been coal-fired (see Plate 4) although the Americans used gas-fired furnaces. The fire-clay pots, which had to withstand great heat, required great skill and care in their making and the trade was often carried on in one family for many generations.

Once lit, the furnace would operate continuously day and night until it was necessary to let it out to replace the pots which had become damaged. Once the ingredients of the metal had fused and the glass was in a molten state it was ready for pressing. Each pressing machine was operated usually by a team of seven known collectively as a chair – there were a gatherer, a presser, a melter and four boys. A 'gather' of metal was taken from the pot on the end of a rod (called a punty) and brought red-hot to the press, which when working was kept at a temperature near to that of the glass to prevent any sudden cooling. The glass was allowed to drop from the punty into the mould, and when the presser judged that enough had entered the mould he would cut off the remainder with sharp metal shears and immediately operate the press with his other hand, bringing down the plunger which would force the glass into all parts of the mould. The plunger was operated by either a lever or a screw action. It will be seen that skill was required to judge the right amount of metal – too little and the article would fail to show the full impression of the mould; too much and the plunger would fail to 'bed' properly, producing at best a thick-bottomed article. Once the plunger had been rammed home it was released, the outer mould opened and the article removed. At this stage it would be at red heat, with a roughened surface caused by contact with the mould and possibly with projecting 'fins' of glass (see Plate 5) where the mould lines had been.

The next stage, called fire polishing, removed the 'fins' and gave a smooth, brilliant finish to the article. In the early days of pressing, the base of the article was attached to a punty by means of a blob of molten glass. The article was then held in the mouth of a small furnace known as a glory hole and reheated while being rotated by hand. This melted the 'fins' and the rough surface, leaving a smooth finish. Care had to be taken not to overheat, which would have caused loss of definition in the pattern. Early glory holes were coal-fired, but later oil-fired ones were used which made the work quicker. About 1850 a sprung metal clip was introduced to hold the article on the punty instead of hot glass. It was the latter practice

5 Close-up of a basket from plate 2 showing a 'fin', the thin sheet of glass extruded along the mould line and normally removed by fire-polishing.

6 Base of an early pressed goblet showing pontil mark where it was attached by hot glass to a metal rod for fire-polishing.

which accounted for the 'pontil mark' on the bases of early pressed goblets, showing where the punty had been detached after fire polishing (see Plate 6).

One of the properties of glass is that it is a poor conductor of heat. If hot glass is allowed to cool too quickly the outside will cool more rapidly than the inside, which will set up stresses and strains in the glass causing it to be unstable and liable to fracture suddenly. It is essential, therefore, that newly manufactured articles are allowed to cool slowly and in a controlled manner, to avoid setting up these stresses. This slow cooling process is called annealing. There were two methods of doing this in the nineteenth century. In the first the pieces, after fire polishing, were put in the mouth of a long tunnel which was near red heat at its entrance and at room temperature at its exit. The goods were conveyed slowly along the tunnel on a train of small iron trucks, sometimes taking twelve hours for the journey. In the second method the goods were placed in a kiln kept at near red heat until it was full. It was then sealed and the fire allowed to die out slowly over many hours, to produce the same result.

7 Tumbler, *c.* 1850, with very thick walls at the base tapering towards the top. Sometimes called a 'deception glass', as it would hold much less liquid than would be apparent from its size.

After annealing, any further work necessary was done before the glass was ready for dispatch. In the 1880s pressed glass was often embellished with some minimum amount of either cutting or etching (see Plate 8), which of course added to the cost.

The pressing of glass in England started in the Midlands with such firms as T. Hawkes and Co., Rice Harris and Co. and Guest, Dudley and Guest. Rice Harris and Co. in particular improved on the early methods and built up a large pressed-glass tableware industry, though in the late 1850s the Midland manufacturers, who were using an expensive lead glass, were to be ousted from the top of the market by the Tyneside manufacturers who used a cheaper glass (see Chapter 2). In 1849 Apsley Pellatt, a well-known London glass manufacturer, made the following comment in his *Curiosities of Glass Making*:

8 Two small cream jugs bearing Sowerby marks, the left one showing the addition of hand-engraved star decoration and the right one the use of etching for additional decoration.

The invention of pressing glass by machinery has been introduced into England from the United States of America. It has not, however, realised the anticipation of manufacturers, for, by the contact of the metal plunger with the glass, the latter loses much of the brilliant transparency so admired in cut glass, hence it is now chiefly used for common and cheap articles. The process of rewarming or fire polishing after the pressure has somewhat remedied this defect.

In spite of this rather *depressing* comment the method had found favour with the Midland trade, and a report on the Great Exhibition of 1851 makes favourable mention of the pressed glass of Rice Harris in particular.

Rice Harris and Sons' pressed glass is of the greatest interest. By pressing into moulds this elegant material is produced to the public in useful and symmetrical forms, at prices considerably below those at which cut flint glass could possibly be offered. Many of the specimens of pressed glass exhibited have a degree of sharpness in all the ornamental parts, which render it difficult without a closer examination to say whether or not they have been subjected to the operation of the glass cutter's wheel.

Also at the Great Exhibition a new application of the pressing process was shown by Messrs Powell and Sons of the Whitefriars Glassworks, who exhibited their patent pressed glass for windows. The pattern was pressed in the glass, and in a subsequent process glass of another colour was run into the pattern. The whole thing was then ground down to a uniform surface and polished.

The range of pressed items at the Exhibition was considerable and included tumblers, goblets, wineglasses, sugar basins, butter coolers, salt cellars, honey pots and door and drawer knobs – this last item being one of the earliest pressed-glass articles produced in the nineteenth century in America or England. A writer in 1887, reviewing the last fifty years of the glassmaking trade, appeared to be no lover of pressed glass and made the following comments:

The first pressed glass dishes were probably introduced by Rice, or Bacchus and Green, or Hawkes. They were square and pillared in pattern and a 10-inch sold for 3s 6d. Now what has pressed glass done for us? It is cheap; we wish we could say it were better.

9 Early pressed goblet, *c.* 1850.

Most certainly, with few exceptions, the design is as bad as the glass.

How changed is pressed glass during half the period named at the head of this article! Butters round and in three pieces were unknown; two-piece butters, as well as oval butters were an introduction, a quarter of a century ago, by Sowerby's Ellison Co. Pressed tumblers were invented by Harris thirty-five years ago; so were heavy salts and sugars; but it is only fair to say that Bacchus and Green followed closely if not more cleverly, at his heels, for their pressed dishes, etc. might be reintroduced in our day. Pressed glass then fetched a good price and was made with brilliant crystal. (See Plate 11.)

10 Pressed cream jug, *c.* 1850.

11 Small compôte and tankard showing 'pillar' design, *c.* 1860.

The question of industrial relations has already been mentioned in connection with the development of the British pressed-glass trade in the nineteenth century. To discuss the problem in detail would take too long, but a few comments and quotations from contemporary documents will highlight some of the problems and attitudes that affected the situation. Basically the employees and the masters were at loggerheads throughout the period on the questions of rates of pay, speed of working, method of working, and the number and type of men employed. The question of drunkenness also comes into the picture from time to time, as does comparison between the attitudes of men in Britain compared with their fellows on the Continent *and* in the United States.

The men were represented by various unions such as the Glass Blowers' Society, the Pressed Glass Makers' Society, the Flint Glass Workers' Association and the Glass Makers' Society. Most of them had been founded originally to assist members financially in cases of unemployment, sickness or death, and were not involved with relations between management and employees. But in the 1850s these societies gradually became involved in the management side of the business, which was regarded by the employers as an interference which they were not prepared to tolerate. What followed was the great 'lock-out' of 1858–9 which benefited neither employer nor worker, since production ceased altogether. The deadlock was broken by the introduction of a code of mutually agreed rules, which amongst other things restricted the number of apprentices that could be employed. The lock-out had affected the whole of the glass trade, but the root cause of the problem as far as the pressing men were concerned was that the introduction of the pressing machine enabled goods to be made very much more quickly and by less skilled men. This meant that for the same output fewer men were required and, not needing to be so skilled, could expect to be paid less. The response of the workers to this was to restrict output from the presses to that which could be achieved by the blow-moulded method, and to oppose any reduction in wages. Furthermore, good workers were not allowed to be advanced at the expense of poor workers. If there was a vacancy in a particular grade no worker in a lower grade could be raised to the position if there was a man of that position unemployed, no matter how poor a worker he may have been, or the reason for his being unemployed – which could well have been ineptitude or drunkenness.

There were variations on this theme, and as always compromises were reached. Nevertheless the industry failed to expand and realise its potential, bearing in mind the demand for cheap pressed goods from the increasing population. The reasons for this failure would appear to be that the restrictive practices made pressed glass in Britain non-competitive in world markets, and the trade went to the Continent and America. Two reports in the *Pottery Gazette* in 1884 highlight the problems:

> Unfortunately, however, since the year 1865 more particularly, the foreigner *has* slowly but gradually encroached upon the English glass trade, principally in the cheaper classes of goods, where the quantities are large and the labour required in production not highly skilled, such as publican's glass, chimneys, etc. Of course this has not been the work of a year but has continued slowly since about the time I name. The English manufacturer, as the foreigner has encroached on his trade, has by necessity been compelled to use his ingenuity in bringing out novelties by which he could keep his men employed, so that the operatives did not experience the effects of this competition until the severe depression of 1877, when their numbers employed declined from 1,778 to 1,542 and 1,452 in 1880.

In the December issue of the same year, in an article entitled 'Some Reasons Why We Are Undersold by Foreign Glass Manufacturers', we find the following:

> On the Continent, if a man is a poor workman he gets smaller wages, this being a question between himself and his employer according to his ability. In England, supposing a man comes to work – say a wine workman – who is an unsteady, idle workman, who does not earn a week's work in eight turns, he starts at the same rate of wages, under the same conditions and numbers as his neighbour (who is perhaps an industrious, clever, steady workman), who in the same time makes two weeks' wages, and of course there is no comparison between the two. Yet the number of articles required in the eight turns cannot be increased because the poor workman could not then earn his wages. How different on the Continent! There the good workman would have his wages raised, while the poor workman would either have to work for a smaller wage or leave. Again, a man who is not a competent

workman and who does not produce a full quantity of work per week, takes up room which might be utilized by a clever workman; and still if this man is sent by the Glassmaker's Union he must be employed. The Continental manufacturer may have as many apprentices as he likes, and if a young man is clever he is advanced: not as here, where we cannot put on an apprentice if there is a journeyman out of employment, until we have tried him, although we know he will not suit. Of course this increases the number of competent men, and thus tends to raise both the standards and the competition of the workmen. In fact the weakest goes to the wall. In England we are allowed only a limited number of apprentices; and these are only allowed to be bound if there are no journeymen out of work. I am sure that the Glass Maker's Union have lots of men on their books drawing money under the head of 'unemployed', who would not be employed for any length of time in any glass works, and they are unemployed not from shortness of work (in many cases) but because glass manufacturers will not light and work a furnace and place eight or nine such chairs on it, who altogether produce perhaps as much work as three or four competent and clever men do, occupying half of another furnace.

Drunkenness was a considerable problem in this as in some other trades, and it was something that the unions were not prepared to defend – although there was perhaps some excuse for an extra intake of fluids in men who worked in such hot conditions. At a meeting between the Midland Flint Glass Manufacturers' Association and representatives of the Flint Glass Workers' Association in May 1887, the employers were complaining about the loss of production due to drink. In reply it was suggested that the employers should discharge workmen who neglected their work through drink, and if they did so they would be supported by the men's society. An American glass manufacturer of English descent, James Gillinder of Philadelphia, wrote also on the same subject:

I wish I could impress upon the English workman the advantage he would gain by avoiding the drinking custom; in quite a good many who have come to this country, this has been the hindering cause of their success. Those who have come with the intention to work, and who have left the drink alone, have done well. American glass manufacturers will not tolerate drunken glassmakers;

from what I have seen of some that come I fear it is a great evil amongst them at home. I believe that the English people can do almost anything they undertake to do, and if they will take hold of this matter in the right way, glassmakers will not be annoyed by being served with foreign made glass.

To anyone further interested in the industrial relations aspect of the subject the pages of the *Pottery Gazette*, 1878–90, will provide many items of interest. I will end this chapter with one further quotation from that source, which appeared at the end of the century in May 1897:

Certainly we have much to fear from Germany and Belgium; they have conquered us entirely; we have nursed the glass trade for its protection until there is little to protect and we would caution other trades to take warning by the present state of the glass industries of England – which are reduced to a state so abject as to have one man in every three idle, although the number of hands has decreased the last fifty years.

Where we have failed in glass making is not from the want of talent but from adaptability; we have not adapted our labour and make to the wants of the community, nor have we adapted our make to the improvements of the time in common goods consumed by the million.

CHAPTER 2

COLOUR, FORM AND DESIGN

GLASS, chemically, is a mixture of silicates. It is made principally from sand with the addition of some of the following: potash, soda, lime, magnesia, lead, iron and alumina. The main constituent of sand is silica which, under the right conditions, will react with the base elements mentioned to produce various silicates. If silica is mixed with soda at ordinary temperatures nothing happens, but when heated there is a vigorous chemical reaction. Similarly if silica is mixed with lead oxide (litharge) and heated, a chemical reaction takes place. In the first case soda glass is formed, and in the second lead glass.

Lead glass, usually referred to as flint glass, is chiefly used in domestic and ornamental glassblowing. It is more brilliant, colourless and transparent; it is also considerably heavier and more expensive than soda glass.

The early Midland pressed-glass trade used lead glass in its productions, while one of the reasons for the later ascendancy of the Tyneside trade was its use of a semi-lead glass, which used soda potash or baryta as well as lead in its construction, and was cheaper than the pure lead glass. Some glasshouses, in the 1880s, used a pure soda glass as it was cheaper, but it was unsatisfactory since it was not hard-wearing in general domestic use. Soda glass – also known as lime glass – was used far more on the Continent and in America for pressing.

It is important in domestic and ornamental glass that the sand should be as free as possible from impurities. The glasshouses of Venice were said to have been supplied with sand from the coast of Syria which had been famed for its excellence since the days of ancient Rome. In the nineteenth century in England the sand for pressed glass came either from Alum Bay on the Isle of Wight or from France, in particular the region around Fontainebleau, in the latter case at high prices. The chief impurity found in sand is some form of iron oxide which gives a green colour to the glass. This is often seen in bottle glass where the colour is not significant. The green coloration can be removed by adding a small quantity of manganese oxide to the batch. This was a difficult process since the amount of iron varied, and too much manganese would result in a purple colour which accounts for the faint purple hue sometimes seen in nineteenth-century pressed glass. Later, arsenic was found to serve the same purpose and to be more manageable.

Occasionally in pressed glass one finds small lumps of a white substance not unlike soda in appearance (see Plates 12 and 13).

12 Goblet, *c.* 1850. Note mould lines on the foot.

13 Close-up of rim of the goblet in plate 12 showing the presence of 'stones', due in this case to a poor batch mix.

These were called 'stones', and originally attributed to a defective glass mixture. However an authority of the day, Professor Barff, wrote in April 1876: 'On microscopic examination I found that the white substance is a glass and crystalline and by analysis that it contains alumina. I have no doubt that the pots used for melting are at fault.' In other words the alumina which is part of the constituents of the clay used in making the pots could under certain conditions be deposited into the molten metal. Professor Barff went on to say that careful attention to detail in the manufacture of the pots and care in their use could go a long way to eliminating this defect.

Later research showed that both types of stones occur. Those arising from the glass mixture are called 'batch stones' and those arising from the pots are called 'clay stones'. The two types can often be distinguished from each other by the fact that the former frequently are surrounded by a mass of minute bubbles of gas whereas the latter are not.

So much for the production of colourless glass, which for ease of reference is usually referred to as flint glass to distinguish it from coloured glass, although the term strictly refers to a lead-containing glass.

Coloured glasses are produced by using various metallic oxides rather in the manner of porcelain enamel painting. Charcoal and sulphur are also used. Glassmakers differed considerably in their recipes for the various colours, of which there were a large number. The colours produced by metallic oxides vary according to the nature and quantity of the oxide used, the glass mixture to which it is added and whether or not there is a reducing or oxidising agent present. A reducing agent is one which removes oxygen from a chemical, whilst an oxidising agent adds oxygen to it.

Cobalt oxide gives a beautiful dark blue colour and manganese a purple or black colour, depending on the quantity used. Manganese can also be used in conjunction with iron and arsenic to produce a variety of shades of amber. Ferrous (iron) oxide produces an olive green or a pale blue, according to the glass with which it is mixed. Ferric oxide gives a yellow colour but requires the presence of an oxidising agent to prevent reduction to the ferrous state. Copper gives a peacock blue colour which becomes green if the proportion of copper oxide is increased. Gold is used for the production of red or ruby glass and seems to produce its best effect in a lead-containing glass. Uranium is used to obtain a fine yellow colour, and in the absence of a large percentage of lead will also render the glass fluorescent. Similarly, finely divided charcoal (carbon) added to soda glass gives a yellow colour, and by increasing the proportion of charcoal the intensity of the colour can be increased until it reaches black opacity. Other black glasses, while appearing black by reflected light, often show beautiful blue, purple and green colours by transmitted light, depending on the colouring agent used.

With the exception of charcoal black, the colours mentioned so far have all been translucent. Opaque and opalescent effects can also be obtained. A double silicate of sodium and aluminium, known as cryolite, was usually used for this purpose – it could produce effects varying from opalescent to opaque white. The latter could be coloured with the appropriate metallic oxide. Another chemical sometimes used to give opaqueness to glass was calcium sulphate. The opacity was caused not by a chemical combination but by the unfused sulphate trapped in the glass in a fine state. The cryolite came from Greenland and was a German monopoly. At one point in 1885 its importation was threatened by a trade disagreement, but it was discovered that cryolite was not indispensable to the production of opal glass, as some manufacturers had thought. An opal glass equal if not superior to that made with cryolite had been made for some years in Britain, using native fluorspar which was one-tenth the cost of cryolite.

The chemistry of colouring glass was not understood precisely in the nineteenth century, and occasionally unusual colours do turn up which do not relate to any known catalogue colour. These were probably experimental pieces or the result of a batch going wrong.

The popular period for coloured pressed glass was 1870–90, and there was a wide range of both translucent and opaque colours. Many of these were patented, particularly those of Sowerby's Ellison Works (see Chapter 3), who amongst other things introduced the opaque glass known as vitroporcelain, the ivory-coloured version of which they termed Queen's Ivory Ware (see Plate III).

The following colours are found in both opaque and translucent versions – white, black, pale blue, deep blue, yellow, green, brown, red and opaline. In addition a number of marbled effects were achieved, particularly purple and white, blue and white and green and white (see Plates II, III, VI). A popular name for this type of marbled glass is slag glass or 'end of day' glass. The term slag glass was used because slag, which is the scum taken from the surface of molten iron in the smelting works, was used in its manufacture. The term 'end of day' glass is, however, a misnomer, and arose from two misconceptions – one, that the slag was run off from the molten iron at the end of the day, which was not necessarily true; the second, that at the end of the day all the remaining batches of coloured glass were mixed together to use them up, thus producing the marbled effect. This was not true either, since there was no end to the day in a glasshouse. Once the furnaces were lit they were worked on a twenty-four-hour system, with three shifts each of eight hours. In any case the marbled effects were not the result of a haphazard mixture but were carefully worked-out formulae capable of being reproduced at will. They were often given special names, such as malachite for the green and white glass after the mineral of that name.

In 1889 Davidson's of Gateshead produced their famous Pearline glass (see Chapter 8) which achieved great popularity in the 1890s and is being reproduced today, in some cases from the original moulds. Although Davidson's invention was protected by patent, a type of glass suspiciously like it was introduced by the Manchester firm of Burtles, Tate and Co., under the name of 'Topaz Opalescent', which from its description resembles Pearline glass in appearance, though the result may have been achieved by a different method. Similarly, Plate VII shows a rare brown-coloured basket with a Pearline-type finish, the design of which was registered on 3 November 1890 by Greener and Co. So it would appear that not all of this particular type of glass can be attributed to the Davidson Works.

Towards the end of the century iridescent glass was introduced, in which the surface of the glass was treated chemically to produce an iridescent effect. If this was done on deep blue or green glass the result was quite pleasing, but if done on clear flint glass the result was that peculiar orange-coloured glass which was and is so popular with the Americans. It is known as carnival glass (see Plate V) because it was often given away as prizes at fairgrounds and carnivals. In the better-quality work the surface was treated on both sides, but in some cheaper productions only one side was treated. The popularity of this type of glass continued into the Edwardian period.

It often happens that when a new manufacturing process or material is introduced the form taken by its products follows closely at first the current fashions of its nearest relative. In the case of pressed glass early shapes copied those of free-blown and blow-moulded glass and consisted mainly of tableware. Later the advantages of the process began to be exploited and cylindrical, rectangular and square shapes became the order of the day, shapes which showed to best advantage the crisp reliefs of which the process was capable (see Plate 14). Breakfast sets were very popular which, although excluding individual cups, saucers, bowls and plates, often

14 Black tea caddy showing the crispness of designs produced by pressing, *c.* 1880.

consisted of up to twenty pieces and included biscuit barrels, tea caddies and celery vases. The latter often served a dual purpose, for when inverted they acted as stands for large plates, thus producing compôtes.

Like the shapes, the early surface designs followed the contemporary fashion for cut glass. This was an effect easily achieved by pressing and the result, at its best, was capable of deceiving many people. However in the 1850s the fashion changed and cut glass was no longer in demand. John Ruskin was a prime mover in this change of fashion. In his book *The Stones of Venice*, published in 1853, he expounded the view that the natural beauty of glass and its tendency to flow in curves was sufficient ornamentation without the distortion of diamond cutting. As a result etching and engraving became more popular and the use of naturalistic designs more frequent. Pressed glass responded to some extent to the new fashion and also went on to develop designs peculiar to itself. In America in the 1830s a type of design known as 'lacy' had been popular. It consisted of covering the background to any design with a series of small, hemispherical beads which reflected the light and gave a lace-like effect to the finish (see Plate 15). This type of decoration was used in England in the 1860s

15 Cup plate showing 'lacy' design. Registered design lozenge. Henry Greener, 7 December 1869.

and 1870s, particularly on some commemorative pieces where it formed an attractive contrasting background to any inscription (see Plate 46). At about the same time there was a vogue for a combination of clear and frosted patterns on the same piece (see Plate 64). Molineaux, Webb produced a number of these designs. Neo-classical motifs such as the Greek key pattern and the Vitruvian

16 Fine Corinthian column candlestick, typical of the neo-classical designs of a hundred years earlier found on some pressed glass of the 1880s. Unmarked. Height 10½ in (26.25 cm).

scroll were often used in association with this type of decoration.

Neo-classical designs were produced, in some cases copying eighteenth-century designs in silver such as the fine Corinthian column candlestick shown in Plate 16. A number of pieces, which although unmarked have many features in common and may be from the same factory, are found showing swags, ram's heads, caryatids and other neo-classical features (see Plates XI and 17). These may have been intended for a more sophisticated market than the bulk of pressed-glass designs, which were intended for the homes of the working classes. Familiar themes such as nursery rhymes were produced by Sowerby Ellison Works (see Plate 24). Nationalistic emblems such as the rose, shamrock and thistle were used, particularly on commemorative pieces depicting royalty and national figures. The lion of England is found modelled by at least two factories, Henry Greener and John Derbyshire – who also produced a model of Britannia (see Chapter 9 and Plate IX).

In the late 1870s and 1880s many naturalistic designs appeared using vines and other vegetation, shells, fishes, etc. (see Plates 69

17 Black vase showing a mixture of features from 18th- and early 19th-century designs, including 'swags', 'lion mask monopodial supports' and 'Greek key' pattern, c. 1880.

and 70). Three-dimensional models were produced of familiar things such as dogs, cats, and Punch and Judy for use as fireside ornaments or paperweights. Many of these designs were produced by the glasshouse owners themselves. Thomas Davidson of George Davidson and Co. and J. G. Sowerby of Sowerby Ellison Works were particularly renowned as men of artistic ability who produced original designs. Some ideas were taken from contemporary artists and sculptors, such as Landseer's lions (see Plate 60) and Kate Greenaway's figures (see Plate 23).

Apart from a large range of containers for table use, pressed articles were produced in abundance for the Victorian parlour and elsewhere – pin trays, cigar trays, spill holders, flower holders, inkwells, candlesticks, chamber sticks, nightlight holders, match holders and small baskets of various kinds for both decorative and functional purposes.

In the 1880s the addition of etching and engraving to the pressed glass came into fashion again after a lull of some fifteen years, particularly at the Sowerby Ellison Works. Ferns and other designs were etched and engraved into the glass, sometimes including inscriptions commemorating local events such as fairs; inscriptions would often be added to a standard design as and when required. Many of these small glass novelties were known as penny goods and literally sold for one penny each (see Plate 71). By the end of the century the demand for novelty goods had abated somewhat and with it the demand for coloured glass generally. In their place the fashion for cut glass began to make a comeback. The pressing houses were not slow to take advantage of this reaction and reverted to their original role of producing pressed glass in imitation of cut glass. Technical advances over the years ensured that the new pressed 'cut glass' was even better and more like the real thing than the earlier examples had been. The necessary mould lines were concealed within the cut design, often following a zig-zag path through the pattern.

In the early 1900s the bulk of the pressed-glass output consisted of tableware of various types and toilet sets for dressing tables. The latter usually included a tray with a powder bowl or hair tidy, a pair of small candlesticks, and a ring stand or saucer. Opaque coloured glass had largely gone out of fashion, and the only translucent colours that were used were pale pastel shades of pink, blue and green.

As well as the large range of domestic designs a number of commercial items were produced by pressing, including pavement lights (see Plate 18), which were large rectangles and squares of thick glass set in pavements to provide light in underground rooms. Glasses for colliery lamps were also pressed, as were many varieties of glass covers for ship's lights – port, starboard and masthead.

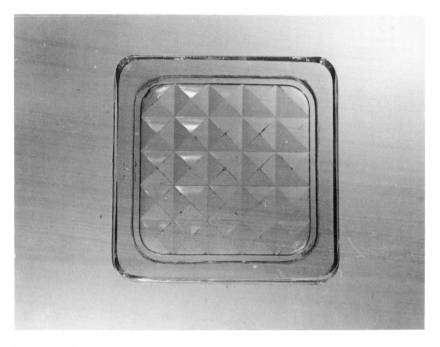

18 Pavement light used for illuminating underground rooms, *c.* 1890.

CHAPTER 3

THE SOWERBYS OF GATESHEAD

GATESHEAD in the early nineteenth century was a small town on the south bank of the river Tyne, opposite the larger town of Newcastle. It became during the course of the century the chief place in England for the manufacture of pressed glass, and by far the largest glasshouse in the area was that owned by the Sowerby family.

The earlier history of the family is not known precisely, but it would appear that George Sowerby came to Gateshead from the neighbouring area of Redheugh, where he already had a glassworks, in about 1765. He probably moved to be nearer the centre of glass-making activity, which would be more convenient for labour and fuel. He settled in Pipewellgate, the glass-manufacturing area of Gateshead, where he built two separate glasshouses which he ran very successfully. He made general glass goods by the free-blown and blown-moulded processes before very much in the way of cut glass was being produced.

His son, John, who was to carry the business forward to become the greatest pressed-glass manufactory in the country, joined his father in the business in the early 1820s. He assisted in the management of the works as well as travelling for the firm to boost their sales – a tedious task in those days without the railway to carry him or the goods he sold. In later years he was to recall the rigours of a three-hundred-mile journey to London on the outside of a stagecoach.

The Pipewellgate Works was known as the New Stourbridge Works, perhaps alluding to the type of glass being made there. The Sowerbys also owned near-by Broomhill Colliery, and so a good supply of coal was ensured for their single furnace, which housed twelve pots. About 1850 the firm moved to new and enlarged premises in Ellison Street, in a part of the town adjacent to the North-Eastern Railway which gave them very good access for the delivery of raw materials and the dispatch of finished goods. The new glasshouse had six eight-pot furnaces under one roof, which not only minimised costs but gave added comfort to the workmen. Throughout their history the Sowerbys have been great inventors and innovators, and the new premises contained all the latest inventions and appliances. It was at this time that the production of pressed glass commenced in earnest.

Its introduction into the north-east was by no means a peaceful activity. As early as 1846 John Sowerby had taken over the Gateshead glassworks of a Mr Cook, who had been rendered bankrupt by a dispute with the Glass Blowers' Society, the local union, over rates of pay. It was perhaps not the best atmosphere in which to attempt the introduction of a pressing machine and a new system of payment based on a fixed wage rather than piecework, which was the accepted method in the glassblowing industry. This brought John Sowerby into open conflict with the Glass Blowers' Society on two counts – first, the reduction in wages and, second, the reduction in workforce if pressing were to become the standard method of production, since one man could produce goods at a far greater rate by this method.

Sowerby brought a court case concerning intimidation of his workforce whom he had succeeded in hiring at a fixed rate. Two men were found guilty of intimidation and given sentences of fourteen days' imprisonment. However the wrangle went on. Samuel Neville, a glass manufacturer from the Midlands who had served his apprenticeship with Bacchus and Green of Birmingham, was employed by Sowerby as manager of the glassworks taken over from Cook. It was now known as the Gateshead Stamped Glassworks, and Neville maintained that it had nothing to do with the Glass Blowers' Society since it was intended only for stamped or pressed glass. Neville also argued that with stamped glass the articles were made for the men by the machine, instead of the men having to blow and mould the work laboriously themselves – therefore the men working the presses could work longer hours. This argument overlooked the fact that the physical strength required to operate the press was considerable, and the union was not slow to pick this up. The arguments went back and forth until eventually a solution was found, which unfortunately is not on record. This, however, was not the end of the problems in the pressed-glass industry, which are related in Chapter 1.

In 1855 Sowerby took Samuel Neville into partnership and the firm traded as Sowerby and Neville. They instituted at the works in Ellison Street a small iron foundry to produce the metal moulds essential to the manufacture of pressed glass. During this period, also, three new furnaces were added. The firm introduced many new glass novelties, causing fierce competition with neighbouring glasshouses, particularly the Wright Brothers of Pipewellgate.

John Sowerby became a magistrate, and his time on the bench was marked by sound sense and firmness tempered with mercy, qualities no doubt essential in his business life also, where, as an employer, he was highly regarded as a considerate and just man. During his time as head of the firm nearly every kind of improvement in the pressed-glass trade was perfected either by him or by his equally inventive staff. In these early years he made no attempt to protect himself and his business by taking out patents on his inventions or registering his designs, but by the 1870s piracy of his ideas and designs was so rife that he was forced to take action, and from that time onwards all his designs were registered and his inventions covered by patents. Lists of these can be found in Appendices A and B. In 1874 Samuel Neville left the firm and opened business on his own account, forming the Neville Glassworks Co. (see Chapter 7), and from that date the Sowerby Works traded as Sowerby and Co. until 1882.

John Sowerby died some time in the 1870s, one of the unsung heroes of the Industrial Revolution. I can do no better in honouring his achievements than quote from an article published in the *Pottery Gazette* in August 1888, headed 'Trade Reminiscences, John Sowerby, Gateshead'. The author says, referring to pressed glass:

It is generally thought this description of glass, being moulded, is of little value as an art production, for it is an artistic production, when taste and quality, in addition to utility, enter into its designs.

How is it that artistic and general goods in china and other products in clay do not rank as moulded articles like pressed glass? They are produced from the model in common plaster moulds, while moulded glass is produced from the most elaborate and costly iron moulds – indeed, every piece of iron used in these moulds is an example in ironwork, a study for the critic as well as the artisan. Truly pressed glass makers have never had the credit for their productions to which they are entitled.

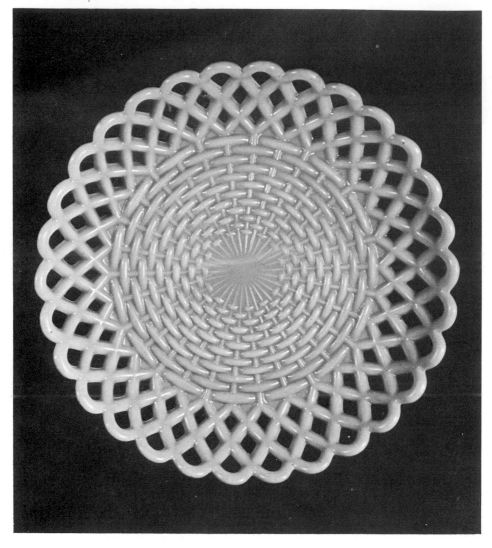

19 Opaque green pierced basket-weave plate which was part of a dessert service, *c.* 1875. Diam. 8 in (20 cm).

Probably had the pressed glass trade been recognised as it should have been, its inventors and designers would have ranked with such names as Wedgwood and Minton; but it must be left to another generation to do justice to the productions in artistic pressed glass – which emanated from the Ellison Glass Works during the fifty years, or nearly so, John Sowerby conducted this and his early works in Pipewellgate.

John Sowerby was succeeded by his son John George Sowerby, who was himself a very competent glass manufacturer and during the 1870s was responsible for introducing a wide range of coloured glass. He also developed the use of colour for stained glass for use in church windows. This part of the business he eventually hived off into a separate company, the Gateshead Stained Glass Co. Ltd, with its own registered trade mark in the form of an owl sitting on a branch backed by the rising sun, all enclosed in a circle. He was a man of artistic temperament and an able designer, who also published two children's books containing his own illustrations, *After-noon Tea* in November 1881 and *At Home* in June 1882. They were described by a contemporary reviewer as 'a charming production and perhaps, as an illustration of childlife – unique'.

John George's son was John Lawrence Sowerby, who eventually left the firm and emigrated to Canada where, it was reported, he set up a glasshouse making similar items to those produced in Gateshead. In 1882 the firm changed its title again and registered under the Limited Liabilities Act as Sowerby's Ellison Glass Co. Ltd. They were not allowed to register the simpler title of Sowerby and Co., since that had already been registered by a firm in Lincolnshire. J. G. Sowerby became the first chairman of the company and the family held most of the shares. Two cousins of J. G. Sowerby –

20 Flower trough in the shape of a boat, Rd. No. 42947, registered 1886. Sowerby mark. Length 12 in (30 cm).

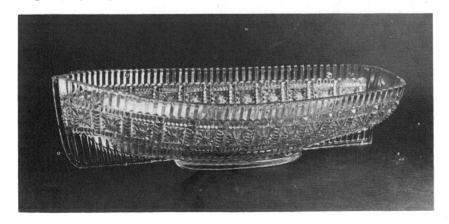

George and John – left the company in 1887 and set up business with Henry Pitt at the old Leamington Glassworks in Newcastle, formerly the property of the Duke of Northumberland. Ironically, because they did not register the company they were able to trade as Sowerby and Co., and their first advertisement described them as 'manufacturers of pressed and blown glass of every kind in flint and colours also cut and engraved' (See Chapter 7). Whether or not there was a family feud going on is not certain, but the new company obviously caused embarrassment to the parent firm who were compelled in their advertisement to include the words: 'The Company especially call attention to their address and title.'

Whatever may have been the family feeling, the workmen at Sowerby's Ellison Works were obviously quite attached to one of the cousins, George, as evidenced by a report in the *Pottery Gazette* in September 1887: 'A handsome hall timepiece was presented recently to Mr George Sowerby of the Leamington Glassworks, Newcastle with the following inscription "Presented to Mr George Sowerby Esq. by the employees of Sowerby's Ellison Glass Works Ltd. as a mark of their esteem".'

21 Brown glass shoe flower holder. Sowerby mark, *c.* 1885. Length 7 in (17.5 cm).

By this time the Ellison Works had offices in Gateshead, Birmingham, London, Paris and Hamburg and advertised their goods 'for the markets of the world'. The family tradition at the works was carried on by the Rev. R. S. G. Green who was a son-in-law of J. G. Sowerby; he became a director of the business but took no active part. The firm is still in business today under the same name.

Following that brief history let us now look at the firm and its products in greater detail. A report from the *Newcastle Daily Chronicle* of 21 October 1882 gives a very clear picture of the size of the works and its range of activities:

> The Ellison Street Works are the largest pressed glass manufactory in the world. They cover an area of five and a half acres of ground and from 700 to 1,000 hands are employed in them. They were established at Redheugh about a hundred years ago by the grandfather of the present managing partner, Mr J. W. Sowerby, but for many years the entire operations of the factory have been conducted at Ellison Street. The production at the present time is about 150 tons per week of finished manufactured glass goods, and the materials necessary to make such an immense quantity of the substance may be said to be brought to Gateshead from the ends of the earth. The cryolite spar, used for the manufacture of opal glass, comes from Iceland; the nitre from Peru; the pearl ash from North America; the barytes from Germany; the manganese from Greece, and the fine silicous sand from Fontainebleau, in France. The soda, oxide of lead and arsenic used in the processes are, of course, obtained at home. The factory works continually day and night, all the year round; the hands employed being divided into three shifts of eight hours each. One hour of each shift may be deducted for meals, so that the workpeople labour for no more than seven hours *per diem*. The staple articles of production are drinking glasses of various kinds, decanters, salt cellars, cake and fruit dishes and plates with various objects in opaque glass. To the production of these goods in the manufactory there is practically no limit but the demand and the rate at which they can be turned out of hand may be guessed from the fact that each man working at the moulds can make from 1,100 to 1,200 tumblers during his seven hours work. In the melting room are nine furnaces containing in all 78 pots more or less constantly in use. Each pot holds from twelve to fifteen hundredweight of molten glass.

Apart from one or two historical inaccuracies at the beginning the account is factual.

On 26 January 1876 John G. Sowerby registered the firm's famous peacock's head crest trade mark (see Chapter 8 and Plate 22) for use on all glass articles in opaque colours, although in practice the mark is found on translucent glass as well. The mark, which is found on the inside as well as the outside of articles, is sometimes indistinct and resembles a performing seal balancing a ball on its head. It is frequently found in conjunction with a registered design mark, because from 1870 onwards the firm registered nearly all its designs – a fact which was advertised regularly in the trade journals, with a request for information regarding any infringements of the firm's rights to the trade mark and the registered designs. That some copying of these marks and their products did occur is borne out by

22 Sowerby mark with registered design lozenge showing design was part of bundle number 9 registered on 10 March 1879.

the fact that in 1881 the following comment appeared in the *Pottery Gazette*: 'Sowerby's have reduced their prices on their goods, which have been copied both at home and abroad, in some cases by 35% in an attempt to stop this piracy.'

The firm was responsible for the introduction of many new inventions to the pressed-glass trade. One of their more notable contributions was the invention of a material which they called vitroporcelain because it appeared to resemble both glass and china – the former in its method of manufacture and the latter in its appearance and composition. It was introduced in 1877 and was basically an opaque glass capable of being produced in a variety of colours, the colour extending right through the material (see Plate I). A contemporary writer makes the following comment:

> Some of the articles in turquoise are exquisite in design and colour, whilst their cheapness will, we hope, place them within the reach of those who at present draw their ideas of ceramic art from the contemplation of atrocious highly-coloured specimens of dogs, cows, etc. which adorn their cottage mantel-shelves. We believe that this substance has a great future before it, and that it is capable of very much in the hands of the ironworker, for it is to this handicraft that the design and make are indebted rather than the glassmaker.

In 1879 an ivory version of vitroporcelain was brought out and patented, which they called Queen's Ivory Ware (see Plate III). A complete pattern book – No. VII – produced in 1879 was given over entirely to vitroporcelain.

An interesting account of another Sowerby invention, written at the time, relates how a Newcastle tradesman while on a visit to Paris was attracted by a new form of ornamental glass:

> It was of a rich lustrous milky colour verging in the thinner portions into that 'sky blue' which milk assumes when its vendor has had dealing with 'the cow with the iron tail'. Held up to the light it shone like opal in a hundred delicate hues chief amongst which was a glowing yet tawny gold that suggested the sun shining through a purple mist at evening.

The reference to the 'cow with the iron tail' recalls the habit of certain milkmen of watering down their wares at the village pump. The tradesman purchased several items and returned home in the belief that he had bought the most recent development of French artistic glass, only to be disillusioned by his colleagues who pointed out that the articles had been made on Tyneside by the Ellison Glasshouse – coals to Newcastle. The name given to this dramatic coloured glass was *blanc de lait* and it was introduced in May 1880 (see Plate III).

Various other new colours followed. In 1881 came a very deep red glass which they called rubine (see Plate IV), and in 1882 a glass in imitation of tortoiseshell. Aesthetic green (see Plate I) was another colour produced in the early 1880s and is nowadays rather rare. In addition to this the firm also had a full range of the more standard colours, to some of which they gave special names. Their marbled blue and white they called sorbini (see Plate III) and the green and white (see Plate II) they called malachite, as did most other factories for obvious reasons. One of the rarest Sowerby pressed-glass colours today is yellow (see Plate I).

Sowerby's produced many pattern books; at least thirteen are recorded but unfortunately, so far as is known, only two have survived – No. VII, already mentioned, on vitroporcelain, and No. IX,

23 Purple marbled flower trough with Kate Greenaway figures around the side. Little girls in poke bonnets queueing up to see a bird's nest in a tree. Sowerby mark, *c.* 1880.

produced in June 1882 and entitled *Pattern book of Fancy Goods*. The latter gives a very clear cross-section of the type of goods being made generally in the 1880s and particularly by Sowerby. Not all the items are pressed – some are blown-moulded. They include vases, spill containers, baskets, match holders, posy holders, inkstands, individual cream and sugar containers, etc. Basket-weave designs are popular, some baskets being shown open and some closed (see Plate 2); the closed effect was obtained by pinching together the handles of the basket with a tool while the article was still hot from the press and in a plastic state. This method of working accounts for a number of unusual shapes which obviously could not have been pressed in that way.

Some articles feature figure groups, many taken from nursery rhymes (see Plate 24). They include Old King Cole, Bo-peep, Mother Hubbard, Jack and Jill and Oranges and Lemons, and show a high degree of skill in the production of the moulds. These designs appear to best effect on plain coloured items – on marbled items the

24 Two Sowerby pieces in Queen's Patent Ivory showing nursery-rhyme figures: Jack and Jill spill vase and Oranges and Lemons flower trough, *c.* 1878.

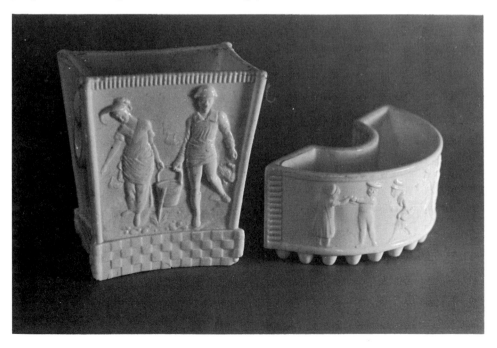

25 Rectangular and semicircular flower troughs used in quantity to make up a dining-table arrangement.

effect is somewhat lost. Flower holders for table decorations were made in oblongs and semicircles (see Plate 25) and were intended to be built up to give a design along the whole length of a dining-table, a feat which could take some thirty or forty individual containers. Swans were very popular and were produced by Sowerby and other factories (see Plate X). They were produced individually as well as being part of a larger design. Stylised flowers and foliage were also used effectively and extensively on Sowerby designs. Overpainting of raised designs in enamel colours and gilding were also used with good effect, particularly on black or white glass (see Plate V).

As well as their regular pattern books, designs were often issued as supplements to the *Pottery Gazette*. One of these supplements, in October 1884, shows how one basic pressed design, say for a sugar bowl, can be added to by means of cutting or engraving to give a whole range of designs. Also shown is a rather attractive design for a money box in the form of a letter box with the words 'Post Bank for Savings' impressed on the side. Designs, particularly etched ones utilising ferns, were becoming fashionable by this time.

In 1887 the production of pattern book No. XII was delayed considerably by a fire at the printers. The complete book, comprising eighty pages and involving many months' work, was completely destroyed together with the drawings and litho-stones. Sowerby's regular advertisement in the *Pottery Gazette* at this time shows an engraving of the factory (see Plate 26), from which one can see the

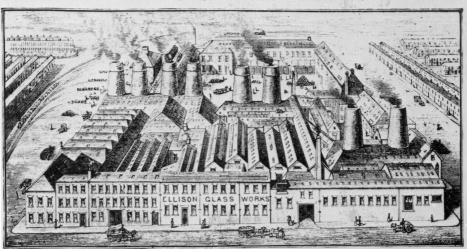

SOWERBY'S ELLISON GLASS WORKS, LIMITED.

OFFICES & SHOW ROOMS:—

GATESHEAD-ON-TYNE. | BIRMINGHAM: 10, Broad Street.
LONDON: 19, Basinghall Street, E.C. | HAMBURG: 49, Gr. Reichenstr.
PARIS: 52, Rue de Hauteville.

MANUFACTURERS OF

CUT, ENGRAVED, PRESSED, & FANCY GLASS

SUITED TO THE

MARKETS OF THE WORLD.

NEW GOODS JUST OUT.

NEW DISHES, BOWLS, AND PLATES, 1896—DISHES, 9½ inches, 4s.; 11 inches, 4s. 9d.; 12½ inches, 7s.   Reduction for Quantities.

26 Sowerby advertisement in *Pottery Gazette* showing engraving of the Works.

vast size of the works and the disposition of the various furnace chimneys; access to the main railway line is also clearly shown.

The year 1887 marked Queen Victoria's Golden Jubilee, and Sowerby along with other glasshouses produced a commemorative plate (see Plate 80). They were not renowned for their commemorative ware, and in fact they made the same plate do for the Diamond Jubilee in 1897 by just altering the inscription.

Yet another success was added to an already long list when in 1890 they brought out their Pea Blossom glass. This was the name given to a newly discovered colour in glass, said to have been made from natural glass. The discovery of the natural glass in Canada had already been reported as 'the most extraordinary geological event of the century'. It was lode material which contained all the elements that formed the different components of glass. It also had a very profitable element in its favour, because it was said to flux with only half the normal quantity of coal being burnt in the furnaces, and was therefore capable of being produced at low cost. Sowerby's Ellison Works were appointed sole agents for the manufacture of items from

27 Translucent pale green bowl with dolphin feet and impressed floral decoration. Sowerby mark, c. 1885.

28 Plate with imitation cut decoration in the centre and floral designs on a frosted ground on the periphery. Sowerby mark, Rd. No. 113560, registered 1888. Diam. 10½ in (26.25 cm).

this material in England. It is likely, therefore, that J. G. Sowerby's son John Lawrence Sowerby, who by this time had his own glass business in Canada, had a hand in these arrangements, although the firm were perfectly capable of acquiring the agency on their merits, being by far the best-known pressed glasshouse in England, with a tremendous overseas trade to all parts of the world.

At one time they opened a factory for pressing glass near Antwerp in Belgium, but this venture survived only a few years. A report in 1888 that they were about to open a factory in Newport, Monmouth-shire, was quickly contradicted publicly by the firm since there was great local jealousy at the thought of a typical Tyneside trade going to 'such an out of the way place'.

Towards the end of the century came the introduction of steam pressing to replace the old hand-operated presses. The method was patented by Sowerby's and came into use in 1894. The new machinery cut the cost of manufacture considerably and helped the firm to compete strongly with imported foreign goods. One advantage of the steam presses was that pieces were turned out cleaner and more brilliant than by the old hand press. This was just one example of the kind of innovation that has enabled the firm to stay in business to the present day.

29 Purple marbled butter dish in the form of a horseshoe showing the underside of the base and the top of the lid. Sowerby mark, design registered 1882.

CHAPTER 4

GEORGE DAVIDSON AND CO., GATESHEAD

GEORGE Davidson's glasshouse was founded in 1867 in the Teams district of Gateshead, and became one of the more famous glasshouses in the north-east of England. Its founder was a well-known local businessman who rose to become Lord Mayor of Gateshead. He was born on 29 September 1822, the son of a miller, at Cow Close Mill in the shadow of Ravensworth Castle. He was one of twelve children and after leaving school he entered the building trade. Later he became a butcher at Low Fell, an occupation which he carried on for twenty-seven years. He was apparently an accomplished singer, greatly in demand at local concerts. He was particularly renowned for his rendering of Tyneside songs and was said to have a fund of Tyneside stories. It was during this period that he first became a councillor and later went on to become Lord Mayor in two successive years, 1886 and 1887. He owned a considerable amount of property in the district, as well as being a shareholder in several companies. His greatest achievement was, undoubtedly, the creation of the glasshouse which bears his name. Starting in 1867 with a handful of men, by 1890 there were 350 employees and the output in terms of finished glass was of the order of 200–250 tons per month.

By 1867 the paraffin lamp was becoming increasingly popular for domestic lighting. It had been considerably improved by adding a glass chimney to restrain the flame and reduce smoking. Initially most of these chimneys were made on the Continent, particularly in Belgium. In his early years Davidson concentrated on the production of these chimneys, with great success. He sold mostly to travelling hawkers who would come and sleep outside the glasshouse overnight and buy the chimneys in the morning as soon as they were cold. There was, at that time, no facility for annealing the glass which was simply put on the floor to cool. This no doubt caused stresses to be set up in the glass – which would reduce the life of Davidson's chimneys and greatly increase his turnover.

Later, as the activities of the glasshouse spread to include the manufacture of wineglasses and small bottles, coal-fired lehrs were installed. By 1877 the firm had four furnaces in production, each accommodating six to eight covered pots each capable of holding six to seven hundredweight of glass. However, by this time commercial changes had rendered the manufacture of glass chimneys comparatively uneconomic and the firm turned its full attention to the production of pressed glassware.

In the mid-nineteenth century one of George's brothers, Joseph, had emigrated to Australia, and in about 1878–9 the two brothers were conducting a very active barter trade. In exchange for glassware sent by George, Joseph was exporting Australian butter, wheat, flour, tallow and bicarbonate of soda. By 1881 George had added herrings and salad oil to his export of glass. Production of all types of tableware had increased considerably and in order to conserve space some articles were packed inside others, which gave rise to some rather odd orders from Australia such as 'biscuits stuffed with mustards'!

Like the Sowerbys, Davidson also used a trade mark at least for part of the firm's life. It was in the form of an heraldic crest – a demi-lion rising out of a mural crown (see Plate 30 and Chapter 8).

30 Davidson's crest trade mark, a demi lion emerging from a mural crown, used c. 1881–90.

The first record of the use of this mark occurs in an advertisement for the firm in the *Pottery Gazette*, March 1880. As far as I can ascertain, it was never officially registered and was discontinued about 1890.

In January 1881 a serious fire at the works destroyed most of the warehouses and processing departments. Although the furnaces themselves were intact the factory was brought to a standstill and over three hundred people were out of work. This resulted in a very strange case being brought before the Newcastle County Court in March of that year, when one of the employees, James Liddel, sought to recover from the firm 'two weeks' wages in lieu of notice, owing to there being no work as the Defendants' premises were burnt down'. Presumably the implication was that the firm were somehow responsible for the man being out of work. The court, however, possibly regarding the fire as an act of God, gave judgement in favour of the defendants but with leave to appeal, since this was regarded as a test case.

In April the firm began rebuilding and at the same time bought up all the stock of moulds and patterns of the Neville Glassworks, which had been destroyed by fire in the previous year. About this time Davidson obviously had some trouble with the Pressed Glass-workers' Society (the local union) as a report in October reads as follows: 'Davidson's have commenced in earnest to recover lost ground following the fire. They have settled all differences with the Pressed Glassworkers' Society and discharged the non-union men lately employed and re-engaged their old hands. They have three furnaces going at present.'

At this time the firm had offices in London, Manchester and Paris and were manufacturing 'every description of pressed glass including vitro-porcelain'. This was the coloured opaque glass first produced by Sowerby some years earlier. Their range of colours included brown, blue, flint and opal as well as marbled effects in purple, green and blue (see Plate VI).

In 1884 a full-page advertisement in the *Pottery Gazette* informs the trade that new showrooms have been opened at the works and that 'Trams run from Gateshead Station every twenty minutes', but by far the most interesting information is contained in the second half of the advertisement:

We have just purchased from Messrs. W. H. Heppell and Co., of Newcastle, their extensive stock of moulds; also recently those of

31 Milk-white covered butter dish showing national floral emblems. Davidson's mark on the base, c. 1880.

the late Messrs. Thomas Gray and Co., of Carr's Hill Glassworks, Gateshead. We also take this opportunity of reminding buyers that we purchased some time ago the whole of the moulds of the Neville Glassworks, Gateshead. These valuable additions to our numerous stock of patterns make it one of the most extensive and complete in the trade.

The same advertisement also mentions that a new illustrated catalogue is available. The firm produced various catalogues but only two are known to have survived, photostat copies of which are in the Victoria and Albert Museum Library in London. Although undated, they appear to have been produced about 1884–5 and from them we can get a good idea of their products.

The range of domestic tableware offered is wide and includes butters with lids (see Plate 31), mainly with coral or leaf patterns, candle and chamber sticks, celeries with a combination of frosting and imitation cut-glass decoration. These celeries served a dual purpose – turned upside-down they acted as table centre stands for large plates, an adaptation in common use by other firms at the time. There was also a whole range of dishes, egg cups, flowerpots, containers for honey, marmalade, jelly and sweetmeats, jugs, matchstands, mustards, piano stands, pickle jars and pin or cigar ash trays (see Plates 32, 33 and 34). Design No. 126 (see Plate 35) was

32 A popular Davidson pattern on a cream jug. Trade mark on the base, c. 1885.

33 Small purple marbled pin tray or ashtray. Illustrated in Davidson's catalogue. Unmarked, c. 1885.

34 Double sweetmeat dish with handles. Davidson mark, *c.* 1888.

35 Black cream jug showing Prince of Wales feathers and national floral emblems. No mark, but illustrated as No. 126 in Davidson's catalogue, *c.* 1885.

particularly popular and is frequently found today – it shows the Prince of Wales' ostrich plumes and the national floral emblems of England and Scotland. It is found in a variety of colours on cream jugs, sugar basins and butter dishes.

The second extant catalogue includes some of the designs purchased from W. H. Heppell, such as the shell sugar and cream (see Plate 70), as well as an interesting covered sugar basin with two dogs, one on either side, acting as handles, trying to reach a terrified cat perched on the lid as a knop. The scene was probably a familiar and entertaining occurrence to the regular customers of this type of ware. Design No. 1 in the catalogue is a whisky tumbler in the shape of an enormous thimble (see Plate 36) with, around the top, the words 'Just a thimble full' – yet another example of Victorian humour. Two other designs worthy of note are a small trinket box with a lid, the whole in the form of a crown, and a sugar basin and cream jug with three fishes intertwined as a supporting plinth (see Plate 69), again a popular motif of the period.

36 A Victorian brown glass whisky tumbler in the form of a thimble with the motto 'Just a thimble full'. Davidson's mark, *c.* 1885.

Davidson's frequently issued new designs in supplements to their regular advertisement in the trade journals, and in November 1885 the firm introduced in this way their 'hob nail suite', comprising fifteen or more different items including comports, celeries, sweets, salts, butters, cream jugs and sugar basins. In 1887 they produced a series of articles for Queen Victoria's Golden Jubilee (see Plate 82) and the following year a further series to celebrate the silver wedding of the Prince and Princess of Wales. From 1889 onwards the firm produced each year at least one new design suitable for a suite of tableware, which they called their 1889 suite, 1890 suite and so on.

In the 1870s George's son Thomas entered the family business and gradually took over control of the firm. He was a man of artistic ability and was personally responsible for about ninety per cent of the designs produced by the firm as well as a number of their successful inventions. We can get some idea of the size of the works from the engraving in one of the advertisements (see Plate 37). It was said to be a model of convenience and compactness and Thomas was responsible for most of the internal design, particularly the packing room which was filled from floor to ceiling with a series of shelves into which large boxes could be pushed in and pulled out like drawers. Thus a large range of different sizes and colours could be kept separately and yet be readily available. It was thought at the time to be a unique system, so one wonders what methods were adopted by other firms. George Davidson's experience of the building trade was obviously put to good use, because wherever possible he advised the use of concrete floors and ceilings, which helped to keep out damp – dryness being essential to the manufacture of glass. The works included a design room, packing room, cutting shop, wash house and finishing room. On the first floor was a mould room where about twenty men were employed on the production of the moulds on which the reputation of the firm ultimately rested.

As with all glasshouses, the works operated on a twenty-four-hour system; there were three shifts – six to two, two to ten and ten to six. Although working in a hot atmosphere, the workers were kept cool by a stream of cold air that was forced into the building by a steam engine housed in the packing room. The cool air served the dual purpose of cooling both men and moulds, the latter becoming extremely hot from the continuous supply of molten metal that was poured into them. Ideally they needed to be kept at a temperature a little below the red heat of glass. There was a system of railway lines

Supplement to the *Pottery Gazette*, April 1st, 1889.

SPECIMEN PAGES

OF

1889 Catalogue

OF

PRESSED GLASS

MANUFACTURED BY

GEO. DAVIDSON & CO.,

Teams Glass Works,

GATESHEAD-ON-TYNE.

OFFICES WHERE SAMPLES MAY BE SEEN:—

LONDON:— | MANCHESTER:—

23, Thavies Inn, Holborn, E.C. | 15, Booth Street, Piccadilly.

37 Part of Davidson's advertisement in the *Pottery Gazette*, 1 April 1889, showing an engraving of the Works.

running round the works which connected with the North-Eastern Railway. This greatly facilitated the collection of materials and the distribution of the finished glassware.

In the early years Davidson's were not assiduous in registering their designs; in fact only three designs were registered between 1867 and 1883, which were in 1877–8 and covered ornamental glassware, a design for a vase and two designs for tumblers (see Plate 38). However, following the introduction of their famous Pearline glass in 1889, many of their designs in this material were registered. Pieces in this material constituted a large proportion of their output in the 1890s, the two most popular colours being blue and a greeny yellow which they called primrose (see Plate VII). Occasionally other colours are found in Pearline, such as brown. There was a big demand for this new material which Thomas Davidson had patented. It was seen at the time as a good example of 'inexpensive

38 A tumbler, one of only three designs registered by Davidson up to 1883. Design registered 23 September 1878. Marked on base with '½ pint', Davidson's mark and registered design lozenge.

39 Brown glass flower vase with Davidson's mark on base, *c.* 1885.

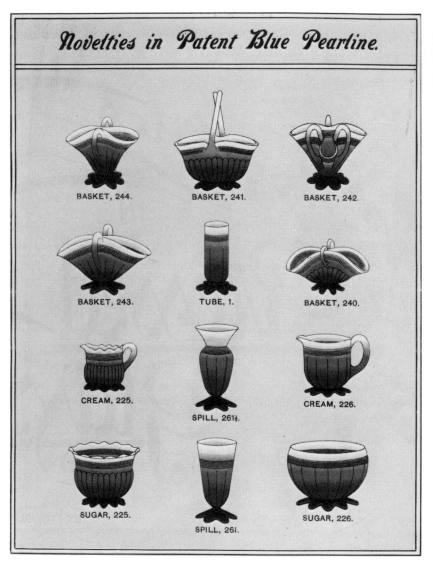

40 Davidson's advertisement in the *Pottery Gazette*, 1 July 1891, showing 'Novelties in Patent Blue Pearline'.

artistic tableware' (see Plate 40). In spite of its being patented it is interesting to note that two years after its introduction a Manchester glasshouse, Burtles, Tate and Co., were able to bring out a novelty glass which they called Topaz Opalescent, but which from a contemporary account of its production sounds suspiciously like Pearline glass. At any rate the result was very similar.

For their 1891 suite the firm produced a pattern which they described as 'the best design we have ever introduced, a good, substantial and very brilliant pattern, special quality glass is selected for these goods; the bottoms of the dishes are obscured by a new process'. The last comment refers to the fact that the bases of the dishes had a matt, frosted finish. The design basically resembled a traditional cut-glass design using a raised octagonal pattern.

On 22 February 1891 George Davidson died suddenly on his way to church. He was sixty-eight years old and had taken no active part in the business for some years. When he was at the peak of his career and Lord Mayor, in 1887, the firm had been awarded a gold medal for its glassware at the Newcastle Exhibition. Success was the result of hard work. When Thomas started working for the firm he began

41 Thick, heavy entrée dish of exceptionally good quality. Davidson mark in centre of base, c. 1885.

42 Translucent pale blue double sweetmeat dish, same pattern as plate 32. No mark, *c.* 1885.

43 Double sweetmeat dish. Davidson mark, *c.* 1890.

work at 6 am each day, the office staff coming in at seven. Even so, they would not finish until about 6.30 pm, and some worked as late as ten o'clock.

The firm expanded considerably in the 1890s and this necessitated more glass being melted. However, the suppliers of the pots in which the glass was melted were unable to produce any of a larger size, and so in 1898 the firm began to employ its own potmakers. As these pots have to withstand very high temperatures their construction requires great skill and patience. It is a craft which is often passed on from father to son through several generations.

Here we must leave the story of a firm which is still in existence today, but let us not do so without one last reference to the skill and inventiveness of Thomas Davidson. In 1910, after some years of experiment, he succeeded in producing his famous flower block or dome which he patented. Many examples of it can still be found today (see Plate 44).

44 The famous flower dome patented by Thomas Davidson in 1910, No. 7830.

CHAPTER 5

HENRY GREENER AND CO., SUNDERLAND

THERE is a long history of glassmaking in Sunderland, and in the early nineteenth century the two most important houses were the Wear Flint Glassworks and the Wear Glass Bottle Works. These two firms eventually amalgamated under the first name. In the High Street at that period were the premises of a glass engraver called Robert Greener, who had married the daughter of Robert Elliot, a well-known local flint glassmaker. Into this glassmaking family was born in 1820, a son, Henry, who was later to become the owner of the Wear Flint Glassworks.

At the age of twelve Henry was apprenticed to John Price, a glass manufacturer of Pipewellgate, Gateshead. He was obviously a successful and industrious apprentice because at the end of this period, at the age of nineteen, he was appointed the firm's traveller. Later, in the 1840s, he took a similar post with the most famous of the Tyneside glasshouses, Sowerby's, at this period also situated in Pipewellgate and known as the New Stourbridge Glasshouse.

In 1858 he returned to Sunderland and entered into a partnership with James Angus as owners of the Wear Flint Glassworks, trading as Angus and Greener. On the death of Angus in 1869 Henry Greener moved the works to the Millfield site where he considerably enlarged them. It would appear, at least from his obituary in the *Pottery Gazette*, that he was a man of remarkable business aptitude and character, an inventor who was always open to new ideas and willing to help others with their inventions. He was a very convivial person with a fund of anecdotes and an ability for quick repartee. He died in June 1882 at his home, Havelock Tower, Hylton Road, Sunderland.

In his will he appointed as his executors three men who had an active interest in his glassworks. They were his son Edwin Greener, his works manager Frank Ord Thompson who had been with him for fifteen years, and his nephew Thomas Scurr who had been the firm's principal accountant for some years previously. The executors were instructed to carry on the business as before in the interests of the family. In pursuance of this aim the executors placed the following letter in the form of an advertisement in the *Pottery Gazette* in July 1882:

> Wear Flint Glassworks,
> Millfield, Sunderland
> 13 June 1882
>
> Mr Henry Greener having by his will appointed us (because of our practical knowledge of his business derived during the many years we have assisted him in its management) executors with full powers to carry on his Works. We beg to intimate that no alteration will be made in the business but that the Works will be carried on as usual under the old name – Henry Greener. All accounts will be received and paid by us
>
> Edwin Ingham Greener
> Frank Ord Thompson
> Thomas Scurr

There is some evidence from the trade journals that the firm had not been doing too well at the time, but a report in October 1882 indicated that things were improving – they had 'relit another furnace and set to work more chairs', and the prospect of a term of prosperity loomed ahead. However this was not to be, and trade continued to be bad until finally the firm were taken over in 1885 by James Augustus Jobling. Jobling was a Newcastle chemical merchant from whom Greener had been buying his supplies of glassmaking materials. The name of the firm was changed to Greener and Co., and alterations were put in hand at the works to improve the facilities and enable speedy execution of large orders. Invitations were sent out to inventors and patentees to submit their specialities for quotation. At this time the Company were producing some six hundred articles of domestic ware in both clear and coloured glass as well as commercial products such as pavement lights and various glasses and lenses for ships, railways, lighthouses and tramcars. Operations were, however, still on a comparatively small scale and remained so until the end of the century. After the First World War the firm forged ahead, expanding rapidly with the introduction of its famous heat-resisting glass, Pyrex.

During the early years, when the firm was owned jointly by Angus and Greener, they began the registration of some of their more original designs, not all of which were in pressed glass. Their first recorded design was for a dish registered in December 1858, followed by a butter dish in August 1866 and a decanter the following January. In June 1867 came a design for a sugar basin with a series of glass bobbles on a frosted ground. Although many of the subsequent designs specified sugar basins they were, of course, not restricted to that article, and would usually be applied to a whole range of tableware as appropriate. A large dish with the June 1867 design is illustrated in Plate 45. A final design, again for a sugar basin, was registered by Angus and Greener on 20 April 1869. Shortly after this Angus must have died, because the next design to be registered is

45 Large dish showing raised pattern on a frosted ground by Angus and Greener. Registration lozenge, design registered 26 June 1867.

46 Sugar basin and cup plate commemorating the appointment of Gladstone as Prime Minister. This was the first design registered by Henry Greener alone on 31 July 1869.

under the name of Henry Greener alone and dated 31 July 1869. This was the famous Gladstone for the Million design (see Plate 46 and Chapter 9). A steady trickle of registered designs followed at the rate of one or two per year, commemorative pieces being particularly popular with this firm. The most attractive of these commemoratives was probably the design produced for the visit of Princess Louise and her husband to Canada in 1878.

In the 1870s Henry Greener built up the range of products which on the domestic side included pressed and blown table glass, cut and engraved flint and coloured glass in blue, green, amber, puce, blue and black majolica and malachite (see Plate VIII). He also patented

47 'A design for ornamenting all types of table glass', shown here on a celery vase bearing the first Greener trade mark and a registered design lozenge, parcel 9, 14 June 1881.

a number of ideas for the production of commercial glass for lighting purposes in railway carriages, lighthouses, etc.

An advertisement in 1879 makes special reference to their 'Roman Tiles or Glass Mosaics'. These were ornamental pressed-glass tiles produced in four sizes, from three to eight inches square, in a whole range of colours, and suitable, they said, 'for general, ecclesiastical and domestic decoration but are especially adapted for window flower boxes, conservatories, sanatoriums and fireplaces, hearths and dados'. The advertisement had a colour illustration depicting a fireplace with blue and white, green and white, purple and white and black tiles arranged in a pattern.

On 29 November 1876 Henry Greener registered his trade mark, which, as with Sowerby and Davidson, was in the form of an heraldic crest but not one, as far as I know, to which Greener was personally entitled. The mark shows a demi-lion rampant facing left and holding a five-pointed star in its right paw (see Plate 48). It was registered for use on all types of glass and had not been used before

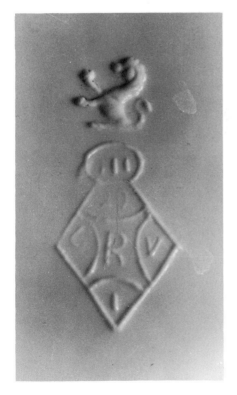

48 First Greener trade mark with design lozenge from the 'grape design' plate shown in Plate 53.

49 Oval dish with floral designs in panels. First Greener trade mark and lozenge, design registered 19 July 1882.

50 Second Greener trade mark, showing demi lion holding a battleaxe, on the 'Victoria' dish shown in Plate 81.

August 1875. The firm did in fact use two separate trade marks at different periods. The one mentioned above was used by Henry Greener and his executors until the firm was taken over by James Jobling, when a new crest mark was instituted. The first reference to this new mark is found in a list of trade marks published in the *Pottery Gazette*, 1 March 1886 (see Plate 50), where it is shown as a demi-lion rampant facing right and holding an axe in its paws.

Careful examination of pieces should make it possible to distinguish between the two marks, although in practice the second mark is usually found facing to the left also.

In April 1887 the firm advertised new designs including some special commemorative pieces for the Jubilee (see Chapter 9 and Plate 81). On this occasion the advertisement included an engraving of the works (see Plate 51). This shows it to have been a large site

51 Part of Greener's advertisement in the *Pottery Gazette*, 1 July 1887, showing an engraving of the Works.

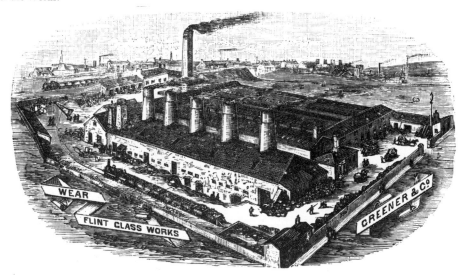

GREENER & CO.,
WEAR FLINT GLASS WORKS, MILLFIELD,
SUNDERLAND,

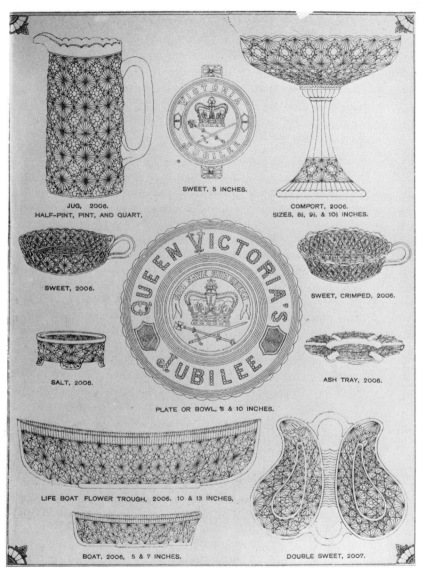

52 Part of an advertisement from the *Pottery Gazette*, 1 April 1887, showing the Greener designs for the Golden Jubilee. (See also Plate 81.)

occupied by a series of long, double-storey buildings; in the fore-ground is the furnace block with five chimneys, one for each furnace. By the side of this is a railway track with a small engine pulling coal trucks. The link with the adjacent rail system can be seen in the distance. At this time the firm had offices in Birmingham, Hamburg and London. The Birmingham agent was Edwin Greener, who had obviously managed to remain with the firm following its takeover.

One of the firm's Jubilee plates was presented to Queen Victoria and was graciously acknowledged. Other designs then in production included their Colonial and Starlight patterns available in a range of sugars, creamers, butter dishes and covers, biscuit boxes, plates, celery jars, salvers, comports, salts, flower troughs (a new design in the form of a lifeboat), a series of jugs and a very modern-looking ashtray. All were advertised as being suitable for home and export. Novelties in penny goods were also being made, but just what these were remains a mystery at present.

At the Newcastle Exhibition in 1887 the firm were awarded a silver medal in the glass section for their pressed glass. They had introduced a new pattern called Royal Star, which consisted of a diamond-cut star encircled with smaller stars used in dishes with crimped or plain edges, and also sugars and creamers. A report of the Exhibition in a Newcastle paper makes very favourable mention of the Greener stand, which was 'loaded with a variety of pressed glass articles of various designs and colours which are either for use or ornament in the household' (see Plates 53 and 54).

53 Milk-white pierced plate with grape design by Henry Greener, registered 23 July 1876. (See Plate 48.)

54 This dish bears the same registered design lozenge as that in plate 53, showing that the design registered was for the border of the plate only. In this case it has been given a rustic finish.

Despite this commendation the firm was not without its troubles. Earlier in the year there had been a 'disturbance' at the works which had resulted in four men receiving jail sentences and another four men being fined. The circumstances were that these men, formerly employees of Greener and Co., many of them trained there, and now unemployed, had banded together to assault and intimidate various Greener workmen to persuade them to leave work or cease to employ or engage other workmen. The reason for their anger was that the firm, in need of more men, had recently gone to Gateshead to engage glassworkers there rather than employ local labour (themselves). For the firm, it was stated that they had a right to go where they chose for their workmen. It was essential to have good, reliable workmen, and these defendants did not answer those requirements and so had been discharged some time ago. The firm claimed that some of their men had been intimidated by the disturbance and had gone home, causing short output from the works of not less than £100 value. After considering their verdict, the bench imposed sentences of three months with hard labour on four men and a fine of £5 each with costs on another four. This is a not untypical case illustrating the clashes that occurred from time to time between the glassmen and their employers and even today, a hundred years later, the story has an all-too-familiar ring.

Following their success at the Newcastle Exhibition further designs were introduced, including a novelty item appropriate to the time, a model of the Eiffel Tower in the form of a candlestick. A

55 Dark blue translucent basket. This bears two different design numbers, one at the base of the handle, which is partly illegible and refers to the handle, and the other in the body of the design, No. 98551, registered by Greener and Co., 21 April 1888. The design has certain features in common with Plate 89.

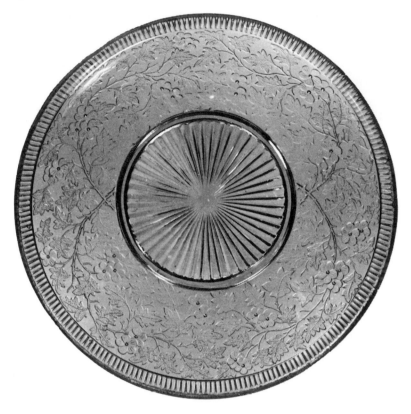

56 Deep dish with floral pattern bearing in the centre Greener's second trade mark, *c.* 1888.

contemporary account describes it as a good design, being a combination of the useful and the ornamental: 'The tower is made in flint and coloured glass and looks very well in opalescent glass.' The same account refers to their Shell and Boat registered designs. These designs were produced in 1889, the year in which the French engineer Alexandre-Gustave Eiffel built his tower for the Paris Exhibition.

In the 1890s the fashion for coloured novelty glass was abating somewhat, and clear-cut crystal was once more returning to favour. Greener and Co. were not aiming at the best glass trade, which went to those glasshouses producing glass by methods other than pressing and in a more artistic and individual manner, but they were trying to supply the best glass possible in their price range. One of their notable designs, introduced in 1894, consisted of overlapping leaves suitably moulded around articles and was a departure from the more traditional cut-glass designs.

It was at this time that the first news was arriving in England of French attempts to produce a heat-resisting glass, but this problem was not to be solved for some years in Britain – not, in fact, until after the First World War, as already mentioned, when Greener and Co. marketed Pyrex. The firm is still in existence, trading as James Jobling and Co.

CHAPTER 6

OTHER MAJOR MANUFACTURERS

THERE were a large number of other glasshouses in nineteenth-century England producing pressed glass. In some cases pressing formed the greater part, if not the whole, of their output. This tended to be so with some of the smaller houses, who perhaps operated only one furnace. They would buy in their artwork in the form of ready-made moulds, and produce a limited range of articles and designs. The larger glasshouses, on the other hand, produced pressed goods in addition to blow-moulded and free-blown glass. Their range would be much larger, as well as their designs and colours.

In spite of registered designs and advertisements detailed information on many of these firms has not been easy to obtain. I have divided them into major and minor factories purely on the basis of their known output in terms of registered designs, trade marks, duration and size of business. The glasshouses were, by and large, grouped in three main geographical areas – Tyneside; Manchester and district; and the Midlands (Stourbridge and Birmingham). Remembering the great use of water for transport in the nineteenth century it will be seen that these three areas – all with rivers or canals – had easy access for fuel for the furnaces, raw materials for manufacture and transport facilities for distribution, not only internally but for world trade via the ports at Newcastle and Liverpool. Of the three areas, Tyneside and Manchester were particularly well known for their production of pressed glass. The major Tyneside houses have already been covered in detail. In the Manchester area the more important firms were Burtles, Tate and Co.; John Derbyshire and Molineaux, Webb and Co.

Burtles, Tate and Co., Poland Street Glassworks, Oldham Road, Manchester

This firm was founded in 1858 and specialised in flint, coloured, ornamental and pressed glass. A number of designs for pressed

I Two spill vases and a flower trough, Sowerby Ellison Works. All three pieces bear the peacock's head trade mark, and the spill vases the registration mark showing the design to have been registered on 14 August 1879. The latter also show two of the rare Sowerby colours, aesthetic green and yellow. Height of vases 3¾ in (9.5 cm).

II *Left to right* Spill vase in unusual blue-green and white marbling, design registered 29 February 1872, but as this piece bears the Sowerby peacock's head trade mark, which was not used until January 1876, it must have been made after that date. Snake-handled basket in rare translucent green colour, design registered by Sowerby 1 June 1874, and the absence of the trade mark indicates that the piece was made prior to January 1876. Spill vase in the green and white marbling known as malachite, Sowerby trade mark only, c. 1880.

III *Left to right* Small pin tray on legs in Queen's Ivory Ware, design registered 13 February 1877. Cauldron in blue and white marbling known as Sorbini, *c.* 1875. Spill vase in opaline glass known as Blanc de Lait, design registered 14 August 1879. Height 3¾ in (9.5 cm). All three pieces bear the Sowerby trade mark.

IV Compôte with detachable stand in rubine glass, bearing the Sowerby trade mark, *c.* 1880. Diameter of dish 8 in (20.3 cm).

V Sugar basin and cream jug in white glass overpainted in enamel colours, design registered 2 December 1879, and a cream jug in orange carnival glass, *c.* 1895. All three pieces bear the Sowerby trade mark.

VI Three spill vases by George Davidson, Gateshead. The centre one has been ground down to convert into a salt cellar, presumably after having been broken at the top. The one on the right is in a rare lavender-blue colour and the only one not to bear the Davidson mark, *c.* 1885.

VII An interesting plate showing two classical Pearline colours by George Davidson: a flower trough in primrose Pearline, design No. 212684, registered in 1893; and a blue Pearline cream jug, design No. 303519, registered in 1897. Also shown is a rare brown 'Pearline type' closed basket bearing design No. 160244, which was registered by Greener and Co. on 3 November 1890. As Davidson's had patented their technique, this would appear to be an infringement of the patent.

VIII Spooner in green and white marbled glass (malachite) by Henry Greener,
Sunderland, showing a portrait of the Marchioness of Lorne and commemorating her visit
to Canada with the Marquis of Lorne in 1878. First Greener mark, height $4\frac{1}{2}$ in (11.5 cm).
(See also jacket, Plate 79 and Chapter 9.)

IX Two figures by John Derbyshire, Manchester: Britannia in green translucent glass, design registered 20 November 1874, bearing the trade mark and design lozenge; and Queen Victoria in an oily yellow coloured glass, unmarked, *c.* 1875.

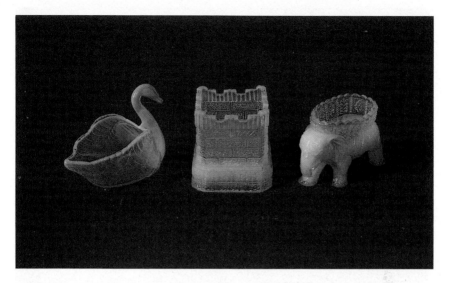

X Three examples of opaline glass: *left to right*, a swan flower holder by Burtles, Tate and Co., Manchester, design No. 20086, registered 1892; a castle flower holder by Molineaux, Webb, Manchester, design No. 29780, registered 1885; and an elephant flower holder by Burtles, Tate and Co., design No. 64234, registered in 1886.

XI Three vases, two with unusual colouring, showing neo-classical features of the late 18th century although made a hundred years later. Unmarked, *c.* 1875.

XII Rare caramel-coloured sugar bowl by Edward Moore of South Shields, design No. 58275, registered 7 October 1886. Height 5½ in (14 cm).

glass were registered (see Appendix A), including in 1871 an ornament in the form of a hand rising from a plinth. The fingers of the hand are spread out so that it could be used as a ring stand. Variations of this design were popular in both glass and porcelain.

By 1881 the firm had two furnaces operating at Poland Street, and had also opened a second glasshouse in Bolton known as the Victoria Glassworks. In the same year they produced a new, cloth-bound, sixty-two-page pattern book with a comprehensive selection of their goods. The firm was expanding its business considerably at a time when the pressed-glass trade generally was going through a particularly difficult period of labour disputes.

An illustrated supplement to the *Pottery Gazette* in March 1883 (see Plate 57) gives us some idea of the range of their products, including pressed items. They made tankard jugs in pint, quart and three-quart sizes, decorated with botanical themes including coconut palms. Sugar basins and cream jugs came in patterns that matched bigger jugs, as did biscuit boxes, butter dishes and marmalade containers shaped like urns. A strange, lobulated covered container seemed to serve a dual purpose as a butter dish and egg stand. The terms 'plain', 'engraved' and 'cut' under the three variations of the design indicate that as well as the basic pressed moulding – which would appear to be far from plain – engraved and cut decoration were added.

In 1885 an ornamental design for a flower holder in the shape of a swan was registered (see Plate X) and produced in various sizes. One of these was purchased by Queen Victoria from a London shop. Although the firm had no London agent they had showrooms at 17 Ely Place, a part of London where many other glasshouses had their showrooms. An advertisement in 1885 indicated that 'Mr Richard Burtles will be in town from the 7th to 18th of September and will attend at the showrooms from 10 a.m. till 5 p.m. daily'.

In 1887 the firm acquired more land near their Poland Street Works, which enabled them to close the works in Bolton and concentrate their business in Manchester by building a second glass-house on the new site, which became known as the German Street Works. Their subsequent advertisement showed a well-engraved illustration of the two sites (see Plate 58).

By 1891 a London agent had been appointed, Mr B. J. Stone, who operated from Ely Place. A contemporary account of the firm's goods implies that they had improved considerably over

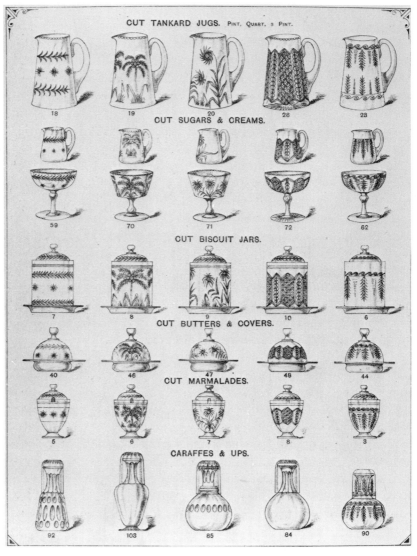

57 Burtles, Tate and Co.'s advertisement from the *Pottery Gazette*, 1 March 1883.

BURTLES, TATE, & Cº.

POLAND STREET WORKS.　　　　　GERMAN STREET WORKS.

Manufacturers of
FLINT AND COLOURED GLASS, ALSO ORNAMENTAL FANCY GLASS.
GLASS NOVELTIES OF ALL DESCRIPTIONS FOR HOME AND EXPORT TRADE.
POLAND STREET, OLDHAM ROAD, MANCHESTER.
LONDON SHOW ROOMS, 17, ELY PLACE, HOLBORN, E.C.　　TELEGRAPHIC ADDRESS: "BURTLES, MANCHESTER."

58 Part of Burtles, Tate and Co.'s advertisement from the *Pottery Gazette*, 1 January 1889, showing both the Poland Street and German Street Works.

previous years and that they had 'a particularly good line in glass flower stands including some new ideas, one of which consists of a tall centre vase and four smaller side vases with a pressed glass fern leaf between each of the latter. It is supplied with either a mirror bottom or standing in a pressed glass dish'. This is obviously a description of the well-known Victorian centrepiece called an epergne. The other novelty which caught the eye of the contemporary writer was their Topaz Opalescent ware which he describes as 'a striking immitation [*sic*] of the old Venetian topaz of the 16th century'. From a detailed description it sounds to me like a 'striking immitation' of the Pearline ware patented by Thomas Davidson of the Teams Glassworks, Gateshead only two years earlier, in 1889 (see Chapter 8). Having seen an example of the colour in one of their registered design swan flower holders, the appearance is hardly distinguishable from that of Pearline glass.

One can only assume that some technical detail of manufacture rendered it sufficiently different not to contravene the Patent Law.

The firm survived into the twentieth century and in 1922 were advertising 'pressed dishes, flower stands, vases in all colours; decanters, waterbottles and wine glasses for ships, hotels and household use'.

John and James Derbyshire

It is difficult to be certain of the exact relationship of these two gentlemen who were responsible for two separate glasshouses in the Manchester area. In the early 1860s the family were trading as James Derbyshire and Brothers of the Bridgewater Flint Glassworks, Hulme, Manchester. In 1870 the title changed to J. J. and T. Derbyshire, and shortly after this it would appear that the family split up, since in August 1873 we find the first mention of John Derbyshire of the Regent Flint Glassworks, Salford, Manchester. The parent firm continued to trade in Hulme as James Derbyshire and Sons.

They registered a number of designs between 1864 and 1876, including a hand on a plinth similar to the Burtles, Tate design. There was a design for ornamenting glass with raised panels of shamrock, rose and thistle and also their Dolphin Compôte which was in the form of three dolphins supporting the raised dish on their tails. The dolphin motif was popular in the 1870s and used by a number of firms in Britain and America (see Plate 69). In all the examples I have seen the creature is shown with scales like a fish.

Perhaps their finest registered design was for a breakfast set with vertical fluting and Vitruvian scrolls. This included a sugar, cream, biscuit box, butter dish, compôte, oval dish, round dish, flower and celery vases.

However, it is the products of John Derbyshire's glasshouse which are better known and collected today. This is largely due to the fact that he used a recognisable trade mark and that he registered a large number of designs, enabling his products to be easily identified.

John Derbyshire, Regent Flint Glassworks, Salford, Manchester

This firm is first mentioned and its first designs registered in August 1873. They consisted of a sugar and cream with a pineapple pattern, and two goblets. From this simple beginning the firm went on to produce a wide range of exciting and imaginative designs from a mammoth's foot serving as a piano rest to a seated figure of Britannia (see Plate IX). The trade mark of the firm is the initials 'J.D.' over an anchor (see Plate 59), which was used from the firm's beginning before such marks could be registered, and does not appear to have been registered subsequently. For many years the mark was thought to have been that of John Davenport, the porcelain manufacturer, who was known to have had a glasshouse and who used an anchor as part of his porcelain trade mark. That the mark is actually that of John Derbyshire is confirmed by reference to the registered design lozenge that frequently accompanies the mark, showing the design to have been registered by Derbyshire.

In July 1874 a recumbent lion design was registered for use as a paperweight. This was based on Sir Edwin Landseer's design for the lions at the base of Nelson's Column in Trafalgar Square in London. As Landseer had died in the previous year it is possible

59 The trade mark of John Derbyshire, 'JD over an anchor', taken from the base of the lion in Plate 60.

that this may have been a commemorative piece (see Plate 60). Other designs based on Landseer's works were also produced, including a greyhound and a large collie (see Plate 61).

Some of the designs were similar to those being produced by other glasshouses, such as a vase in the shape of a human hand holding a container composed of leaves, and a lady's boot for use as a spill holder (see Plate 62). There was also a winged sphinx paperweight; a similar design but without the wings was produced by Molineaux, Webb and Co. (see Plate 65). A covered tobacco jar symbolic of the British Empire was produced, with the seated figure of Britannia on the lid and four panels around the jar with figures representing the four continents in which the Empire was situated. The design was registered in May 1876. Rather more

60 Green translucent glass lion similar to the ones at the base of Nelson's column modelled by Landseer. John Derbyshire design registered 3 July 1874.

61 Unmarked frosted glass dog, *c.* 1875, with plinth similar to lion in plate 60 and almost certainly from the Derbyshire Works.

62 Purple marbled lady's boot for use as a spill holder. Unmarked, *c.* 1880.

common are the pair of figures of Punch and Judy (see Plate 63) which were made in a range of frosted, clear and coloured glass. Finally, Plate IX shows a standing figure of Queen Victoria in classical dress holding a laurel wreath and a scroll. The colour is very unusual, being an oily yellow green, almost the colour of fluorescene. Although unmarked except for the word 'Victoria' around the base, this piece is almost certainly a product of John Derbyshire as it shows so many of the features typical of his figures, particularly in the size and decoration of the base which is identical to the registered design of Britannia shown with it.

The firm changed its title in 1875 to John Derbyshire and Co., and again in 1877 to The Regent Flint Glass Co. No more designs were registered after March 1877. Little information is forthcoming from the pages of the *Pottery Gazette*. The only advertisement to be found is

63 Frosted glass figure of Judy with her cat, one of a Punch and Judy pair. Derbyshire mark on the base, *c.* 1880.

in December 1881, when James Derbyshire and Sons describe themselves as flint glass manufacturers of 248 City Road, Hulme, Manchester and Regent Road, Salford, Manchester – from which it would appear that John Derbyshire had returned to the family fold.

Molineaux, Webb and Co., Ancoats, Manchester

This firm had a flourishing business in the second half of the nineteenth century, operating from their Kirby Street Works in Ancoats, Manchester. Here they had a medium-sized glasshouse working two furnaces most of the time. They produced flint, Venetian and pressed glass, decorated with cutting, etching and engraving. They had London showrooms in Hatton Garden.

The firm began registering their designs in 1864 and between then and 1883 they registered no fewer than forty-five bundles, some containing three or four different designs. On the whole they were for utilitarian articles such as cream jugs, sugar basins, butter dishes, celery glasses, plates, etc. They introduced their Greek key pattern as a registered design in December 1864 (see Plate 64). They also

64 Circular plate with Greek key pattern on a frosted ground. Registered design lozenge, 22 December 1864, registered by Molineaux, Webb and Co., Manchester.

65 Matt black glass sphinx looking remarkably like Wedgwood's basalt pottery. Design registered by Molineaux, Webb, 26 July 1875.

pioneered the use of the part-frosted patterns which were popular in the 1860s. The majority of those registered were for pressed-glass items. One of the best, seen in Plate 65, is for a paperweight in the form of a sphinx. This particular one is in matt black, giving a very good imitation of Wedgwood's black basalt.

Information about the firm is difficult to come by in the trade journals of the time. They did not do very much in the way of advertising, although they did issue a supplement to the *Pottery Gazette* in July 1883 showing their latest Duchess pattern range (see Plate 66). It also shows the return to fashion of cut-glass designs after a lapse of about twenty years.

In 1881 the firm were reported as continuing to work two furnaces and to be fully employed at a time when the glass trade in general was feeling the effect of cheap Continental competition. Shortly afterwards they introduced a new range of items including flower vases, dioptic barrels for lamps and ships' lights.

In September 1882 the following news item appeared in the

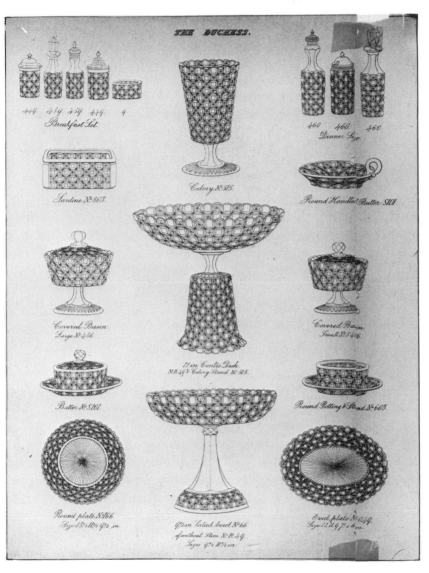

66 Molineaux, Webb's advertisement in the *Pottery Gazette*, 1 July 1883.

distinctive journalistic style of the time: 'A singular accident in July at Kirby St. Works when a bricklayer, who was engaged to build an arch to a furnace, by some means fell into it and was burnt to death. No blame whatever was attached to the firm and the jury returned a verdict of accidental death from burns.' It is an interesting sidelight into the times when presumably it was not considered necessary by either masters or men, in the interests of safety, to put out a furnace while structural work was carried out on it.

The firm continued to register designs after 1883 and Plate X shows an opaline flower container in the form of a castellated tower. In December 1887 the firm became a limited company with a share capital of £20,000, and continued in business into the present century.

In the Birmingham and Stourbridge area there were two glasshouses who played an important part in the introduction of pressed glass into England. Unfortunately it is difficult to identify any of their products today due to the lack of factory marks, registered designs and catalogues. Nevertheless their place in the history of pressed glass is assured. The people concerned in these ventures are Rice Harris and the Richardson family.

Rice Harris, Broad Street Glassworks, Birmingham

Harris was a glassmaker in Birmingham in the early 1830s. He had a glasshouse working five furnaces in Broad Street, which at that time was a rural part of the city. The works began in a modest way under the ownership of three men – Johnson, Berry and Harris – and it was the last of these who survived and did so much for the glass trade in Birmingham. The city was well situated for trade with a canal system in full working order from every part of England. This, together with the nearby Staffordshire coalfields for fuel, gave the city a great advantage as a manufacturing centre. It must be remembered that at this time the railway system did not yet exist.

Harris himself lived in a large house next door to the glassworks, which later in the century became the Children's Hospital. He competed with the neighbouring firm of Bacchus and Green in early attempts to produce pressed glass, and was helped in this enterprise by a man called James Stevens who was a die-sinker to trade and probably one of the first in England to produce moulds for pressing glass. Between them Harris and Stevens were responsible for producing some of the earliest pressed tumblers and salts in the country. These early products were very heavy and thick-walled. Stevens was assisted in his mouldmaking business by his two sons, who later were to manage for many years the mould department of the Sowerby Ellison Works in Gateshead.

Although Rice Harris was a man of undoubted energy and inventiveness he does not appear to have had great business sense. He attributed his financial losses to trying to make glass cotton-printing rollers on which he intended to etch designs with the newly discovered chemical, hydrofluoric acid. He failed in this venture through the simple fact learnt by others, before and since, that glass beyond a certain size and weight is unannealable. This means that it is not possible by reheating and slow, controlled cooling of such massive pieces to remove the internal stresses in the material, which therefore remains unstable. Other ventures which failed for the same reason were glass sleepers, doorsteps and window sills.

It is related that he did not get on particularly well with his workforce. On one occasion, about 1840, he tried to quell a strike at the works by bringing in artisans from France. He lodged and fed them on-site to prevent them being molested, but eventually the English workers won the day and the French returned home.

He made blown goods generally until the advent of pressing, and among his main products were shades for lamps. He frosted and painted them and was the first to apply bright cutting to them. In fact many of the new ideas of this period were introduced by Harris and his staff before the initiative in the pressing trade moved to the north-east. The firm exhibited at the 1851 Exhibition and were the only pressed-glass manufacturers to receive specific mention in the official report of the Exhibition. The quality and cheapness of the new technique attracted particular attention.

The firm eventually closed down in the late 1850s.

The Richardsons, Wordsley Glassworks, Stourbridge

The father of this family was Joseph Richardson, a builder at Wordsley. He had three sons, all of whom entered the glass trade – William Hayden, Benjamin and Jonathan. The most renowned of the three was Benjamin who became known throughout the Midlands as the 'Father of the Glass Trade'. He was born in 1802 and entered the industry as a boy. His first important role was as manager of the Dudley Glassworks owned by Thomas Hawkes, Member of Parliament for Dudley. It was while he was there that he introduced the first glass-pressing machine in England in 1831. The idea was rapidly taken up and improved upon by Rice Harris.

From Dudley, Benjamin went with his brother William to work for Messrs Ensells, Holt and Wainwright at the Wordsley Glassworks, at that time known as the London Glassworks. This was an old-established works even then, and had originally been founded in the early eighteenth century by John Pidcock who was descended from the Hennezels, one of the famous Lorraine glassmaking families who settled in England in the beginning of the seventeenth century and worked under licence from Sir John Mansell, who at that time had a monopoly for all glassmaking in England. Shortly after the Richardsons went to Wordsley the firm got into difficulties financially, the partnership was dissolved, and thus began the reign of the Richardsons at Wordsley.

With Thomas Webb, another well-known name in English glassmaking, William and Benjamin founded the partnership of Richardson and Webb. They ran the firm until 1836, when Webb withdrew to go into partnership with his father and Jonathan joined his brothers in the family business which then traded as W. H., B. and J. Richardson. later on Benjamin became the sole proprietor of the business and subsequently took into partnership Messrs Hodgetts and Pargeter. On the retirement of Mr Pargeter the firm traded as Hodgetts, Richardson and Son, and towards the end of the century the business was carried on by Benjamin's son Henry G. Richardson.

Benjamin Richardson was devoted to his trade and took little part in public life but concentrated all his energies into the development of the glass industry. He was a great researcher and innovator who introduced the process of etching on table and flint glass. He also patented a machine for 'threading' glass and, most important of all, he produced a wide range of coloured glasses including many new colours, among them topaz and chrysolite glass.

The firm exhibited at the Great Exhibition in 1851, and as a result received an order from Queen Victoria for a service of cut crystal for her personal use. They were also awarded, for their cut glass, a medal by the international committee governing the glass section of the Exhibition.

The firm were not much given to registering designs, in fact they only registered one bundle of designs. That was in February 1872 under the partnership of Hodgetts, Richardson and Son, when they produced three designs for flower containers in the form of a witch's cauldron on a tripod, a large swan dish, and a trough shaped like a rowing boat, the outer surface imitating planks of wood.

The family were all extremely long-lived. Benjamin's grandfather lived to ninety-five and his brother William was ninety-two when he died some ten years before Benjamin, who died on 30 November 1887 at the age of eighty-five. In 1897 the title of the firm was H. G. Richardson and Sons, being run by Benjamin's son and two of his grandsons – one of whom was also called Benjamin.

What Josiah Wedgwood did for the pottery trade Benjamin Richardson did for the glass trade, but Richardson did not cultivate the commercial side of his art as he might have done. He made some beautiful pieces – not for sale, but for their own beauty and for the pleasure he derived from making them. At the Wordsley Works were a large number of the most magnificent cameo vases, made on-site and treasured by their owner, who had a special box made for each one so that they could be safely sent to exhibitions in various parts of the country.

CHAPTER 7

MINOR MANUFACTURERS

A S explained in Chapter 6, the division of glasshouses into major and minor is done purely on the basis of their ascertainable output in terms of registered designs, trade supplements and catalogues. This chapter deals with some of the many minor glasshouses which have added considerably to the stock of pressed glass still in circulation from the last century. A few of these firms registered designs but many did not. Occasionally pattern books and trade supplements are available to aid in attribution, but on the whole the products of these manufacturers are difficult to identify with certainty.

Neville Glassworks, Gateshead, 1874–80

This glasshouse was opened in April 1874 by Samuel Neville, an experienced glassmaker who had served his apprenticeship with Bacchus and Green in Birmingham in the early days of glass pressing. He subsequently went into partnership with John Sowerby whom he left to open his own works. The company was founded with a nominal share capital of £75,000 in £50 shares. The whole of the shares were taken up immediately and some £54,000 was called upon when the company was floated.

Although having only a short life it was a reasonably large establishment having four furnaces, containing some thirty-two pots and employing over four hundred men. Little is known about the products of the firm, which was brought to an abrupt end at 10 pm on 1 June 1880 when fire burnt out the entire works.

No attempt was made to rebuild and in April 1881 George Davidson of the Teams Glassworks bought the entire stock of moulds and patterns. A shareholders' meeting was held in January 1882 to wind up the company, and the following year Samuel Neville died at Boulogne in France. In his obituary it was recorded that 'He brought the pressed glass trade from the Midlands to the North of England', and later goes on to say that 'Mr Neville had at one time a large trade but in design and perfection he never reached the character and business of the best houses of the present period'.

Leamington Glassworks, The Close, Newcastle (Sowerby and Co.)

A glassworks had been established on this site for some considerable time, reputedly since 1788. In the mid-nineteenth century it belonged to the Duke of Northumberland and was known as the Northumberland Works. It closed down in 1880 and all that was movable was sold off. The buildings remained idle until the works was reopened in June 1887 by George Sowerby (cousin of J. G. Sowerby) and Henry Pitt, trading as Sowerby and Co., Leamington Glassworks. By September they had one furnace, housing some ten pots, operational, and were reported as being busy. They specialised in pressed goods and claimed that their metal would not change colour in any climate. They opened in a big way, appointing London agents and export representatives and offering a special introductory £4 sample package to the trade, containing a whole range of basic domestic glass.

An illustrated supplement to the *Pottery Gazette* (see Plate 67) shows that the firm's products resembled very closely those produced by George's cousin at the Sowerby Ellison Works. Generally patterns were in imitation of cut glass, but some were engraved with ferns, a fashion which had been introduced at the Ellison Works a short time earlier. In fact the entire supplement follows the contemporary trend in design with little or no originality.

In March 1888 it was announced that the partnership was being dissolved and that Mr Pitt was retiring from business. The concern was to be carried on by George Sowerby who took over all responsibilities for debts and other matters. The following year saw a new line in bowls, dishes, tumblers, butters and sugars, and their advertisement in the trade journal was in the form of a telegram which read: 'To glass buyers, please call at 10 Bartlett Buildings, London E.C. and see out new patterns. – Sowerby and Co.' This at least showed a little originality, which must have then been continued into their products, because in 1890 they were reported as producing goods, 'which, without being copies of those made by older firms, are running them very close as saleable articles. The metal is of good

67 Sowerby and Co.'s advertisement in the *Pottery Gazette*, 2 January 1888. The strong
similarity of these products to those of the Sowerby Ellison Works should be noted. The
cream jug No. 4/50 very closely resembles the left-hand jug in Plate 8. The slight
difference in the shape of the star may have been sufficient to avoid infringement of the
Registration Act.

colour and well finished off'. Four years later they had showrooms in London, Manchester, Bristol and Dublin. They continued in business at least until the end of the century.

W. H. Heppell, Newcastle Flint Glassworks, Fourth Street, Newcastle

It is known that this works goes back to the beginning of the nineteenth century and was at one time one of the largest in Newcastle. In its heyday it was running five furnaces. The original owner and builder was a Mr Wright of a well-known local glassmaking family, who also had premises in Pipewellgate, Gateshead.

Some time after the middle of the century the business was taken over by William Henry Heppell. Although not a great deal is known about the man, his firm is worthy of mention because it registered twelve designs over a ten-year period beginning in 1874. The works specialised in blown and pressed glass in flint, opal and marbled colours. As well as domestic glass they also produced lenses and lamps for collieries and a range of glass for street lights, deck lights and masthead lights. Their advertisements draw particular attention to their cut and engraved moons (glass shades for gaslights).

In 1880 Heppell produced three rather novel designs – a sugar basin in the form of a coal scuttle; a container in various sizes in the form of a coal truck used in the collieries (see Plate 68), which

68 Two colliery coal trucks. The larger in clear glass bears a registration mark and was probably intended for use as a sugar basin. The smaller, in translucent brown glass, is salt-cellar size. Design registered by W. H. Heppell, 19 June 1880.

69 Two cream jugs in milk-white glass. The one on the right was registered by W. H. Heppell, 24 November 1882. The one on the left is unmarked but similar to a design in the Davidson catalogue, *c.* 1885.

presumably could be used for either sugar or salt according to its size; and finally a wheelbarrow with the design imitating wooden planking. Perhaps the strangest of all their designs was the series of jugs, etc. in the shape of fish (see Plate 69), which they registered in November 1882. Used as a jug the result is passable, but when applied to a sugar basin or covered butter dish the result is incongruous and an example of thoroughly bad design.

In October 1884 the firm announced that they were giving up business and in February the following year the partnership was dissolved. Subsequently George Davidson of the Teams Glassworks bought all the moulds and patterns and put them to use. This means that some of the pieces extant bearing Heppell registered design numbers were in fact actually made by Davidson at Teams. Some of the designs were included in Davidson's catalogue, in particular the shell-form milk jug, sugar basin and butter dish (see Plate 70).

70 Sugar basin, covered butter dish and cream jug in milk-white glass by W. H. Heppell, bearing design lozenge, 13 December 1881. The moulds were later bought by Davidson's, and the designs appear in their catalogue.

John Ford and Co., Holyrood Flint Glassworks, Edinburgh

This firm was founded in 1815 by William Ford and remained in the family for over a century. It was best known for its very fine cut glass, but also produced some press-moulded designs, only one of which was registered. This, for a shallow bowl in the form of a pair of cupped hands, was dated 25 February 1876.

A catalogue dating from the 1870s is held by the Hartley House Museum, Cannongate, Edinburgh, which also has a fine collection of this firm's products. A copy of the catalogue is available in the Victoria and Albert Museum, London. It shows among other things some press-moulded compôtes and candelabra supported by figures of maidens, a jug with a lake scene and swans, and a celery vase with a raised fuchsia pattern. They also produced a range of salts, sugar basins, cans and tumblers. Their table service No. 3800 depicts a scene with a long-legged bird, possibly a heron, with an eel in its beak.

A trade advertisement in 1880 describes them as 'Manufacturers in ordinary to the Queen', producing cut, engraved and etched table glass; flower stands and candelabra; cut crystal lamps, gas moons, etc. In the early 1870s the firm enlarged its premises, which were described as the largest glassworks in the north of the United Kingdom. At the end of the century they again expanded their business to cater for the developing trade in electric light shades and globes.

Edward Bolton, Orford Lane Glassworks, Warrington, Lancashire

This glasshouse was started in 1797 by Thomas Robinson and worked as a flint house producing domestic glassware. Later he was joined by his nephew, Peter Robinson. After the death of Robinson Senior the nephew took into partnership Edward Bolton, who was born in 1823. Together they ran the business until 1869 when they separated by mutual consent. Bolton remained to run the Orford Lane Works and Robinson went to open a new works known as the Modd Works at Bank Quay, Warrington, which operated under the name of Robinson, Son and Skinner and was still in business in 1890.

While Robinson was at Orford Lane the pressing of glass was introduced and he made a particular success with a design known as the Empress dish. After his departure Bolton developed the works and took into the business his two sons, George and Charles. Charles emigrated to Australia eventually, but not before he had endeared himself to the workforce to the extent that, on his return to England for a short holiday in 1883, they presented him with an illuminated address recording their appreciation of 'your considerate and courteous manner to all, and also your superior business qualities'.

George remained at the works and records in a letter to the *Pottery Gazette* in August 1885 that he had been with the business 'upwards of sixteen years'. The occasion of the letter was a dispute between the Glassmakers' Union and the Boltons regarding rates of pay for inferior work. The men maintained that the employers were stopping their wages on the pretext of the goods being inferior, and then selling them as best. The Boltons replied that, on the contrary, it had been their custom for over half a century to make an allowance to the men, such as half wages or two-thirds, according to the estimated value of the defective goods. As was usual with these wrangles all the old grievances were dragged up on both sides until finally the dispute was settled.

In spite of these problems the works flourished and Edward Bolton was generally regarded as a good employer. On his death on 26 December 1889 at the age of sixty-six it was noted that a number of his workforce had been in his employ for over thirty years.

Only three designs were registered – in October 1867 a rectangular, fluted covered dish with the word 'Sardines' on the cover; in April 1871 a design for a flower trough in various shapes to fit together to form a long table decoration; and in October 1874 a design for one of the ubiquitous chimney ornaments in the shape of a hand on a plinth. Pattern books were published, with occasional supplements. An engraving of the works in 1885 shows it to have been of considerable size with at least four furnaces working. They had a large home and foreign trade with travellers visiting most of the principal towns in Britain.

Edward Moore and Co., Tyne Flint Glassworks, South Shields

This firm was in business before 1861, in which year they registered two designs for bottles. Apart from a pressed-glass gas globe in March 1868 this was the sum total of their registered designs up to 1883. Thereafter at least one design was registered (see Plate XII).

It was a medium-sized glasshouse operating at least three furnaces and producing both pressed and cut crystal glassware. The firm had the usual ups and downs – on the evening of Sunday, 28 August 1881 their largest cone fell in. Fortunately, although the furnace was working at the time, no one was injured. A year later the firm were again in trouble when they had to discharge forty men. They were accused by the unions of incompetence in organising their works, but the view of the firm was that the union policy of restricting output had led to the redundancies. However things must have improved, because in October 1882 they were reported as working full time with two furnaces ready for relighting.

In 1888 they bought the whole stock of moulds belonging to the Coalborn Hill Glassworks, Stourbridge, which had closed down. The designs of this works, formerly operated by Joseph Webb, were well known throughout the trade and their acquisition by Moore was regarded as a good move. Some of these newly acquired designs were included in the supplement referred to earlier, which shows many flower troughs of various shapes – including swans, an ever-popular form – plates, pickle jars, candlesticks, goblets, salts, knife rests and the usual assortment of sugars, creams and butter dishes. Some of the styles date back over twenty-five years and are obviously from the Coalborn Hill Works.

Edward Moore's works came to an untimely end on 4 July 1891, when the entire factory was destroyed by a fire which started at ten o'clock in the evening. The damage was estimated at £45,000 and four hundred workmen were made idle.

Andrew Ker and Co., Prussia Street Flint Glassworks, Manchester

This glasshouse is of interest because of two noteworthy designs which it registered. The first was in June 1872, when the owners were Ker, Webb and Co., for a pair of flower vases with portrait busts in relief of a man and a woman. From the design representation they look remarkably like the Marquis and Marchioness of Lorne (see Greener's portraits in plate VIII), although no further details are given with the registration. The second design was registered exactly a year later, and was in the form of a covered tobacco box with the word 'Tobacco' on the side. Two other designs were also registered, one for a piano foot rest and the other for a glass dish – the latter in 1876, by which time the title of the firm was Andrew Ker and Co.

Their products included cut, engraved and pressed glass in a variety of colours for domestic purposes as well as lamps and other glass for railway, shipping and colliery use.

In 1885 the son of the owner, Henry Ker, came of age – an occasion duly celebrated by the workforce. It would appear that the son either did not intend or was not able to enter the family business, because two years later it had been taken over by one Samuel Ralphs who traded as 'Samuel Ralphs, late Andrew Ker and Co.'.

Thomas Kidd and Co., Holt Town Glassworks, Manchester

This modest little glassworks, in business during the last twenty years of the century, specialised in glass furniture for birdcages – such things as bird fountains, seed boxes and bird baths. They also produced more mundane items, such as lemon squeezers, brawn moulds, drawer knobs and piano insulators. (The purpose of the latter was to spread the weight of a heavy piano and thus prevent

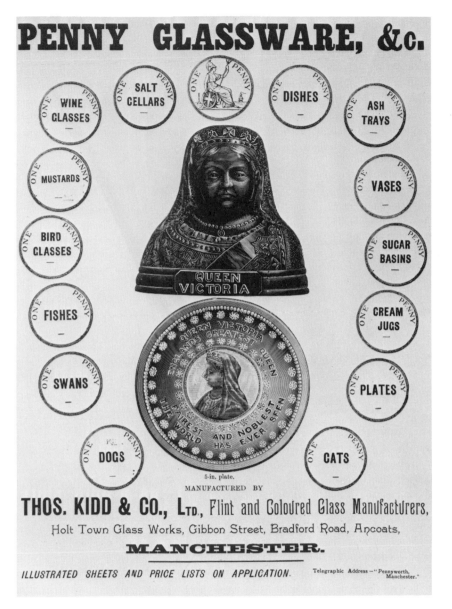

71 Advertisement from the *Pottery Gazette*, 1 June 1897, showing Thomas Kidd's designs for the Diamond Jubilee. (See also Plate 84.)

holes being worn on the carpet.) Their advertisements specified 'a large variety of cheap pressed glass expecially suited for the wholesale trade, comprising salts, plates, dishes, mustards, candlesticks and wines'. Some of these are illustrated in the supplement dated January 1883.

For the Diamond Jubilee of 1897 they brought out two commemorative pieces – one a bust of the Queen and the other a five-inch plate with an appropriate inscription and portrait (see Plates 71 and 84). By this time they were specialising in goods which sold for one penny each, which seems an incredibly cheap price, even for those days, for goods ranging from salt cellars to sugar basins.

The firm may have started business about 1882, because their supplement in January 1883 is sheet No. 1 and it would appear that only illustrated sheets and price lists were published, not catalogues. They remained in business at least until the end of the century. Some coloured glass was produced and also a range of small ornaments in the form of dogs, cats, fishes and swans, although details are not available.

Percival, Vickers and Co., Jersey Street, Manchester

This glasshouse was one of the first to register designs for glass, the first being in 1847 for an oblong dish. At this time the firm was called Percival and Yates. The following year they registered a design for a sugar basin. By the late 1850s Mr Vickers had joined the firm, which then traded as Percival, Yates and Vickers until the early 1870s when they became Percival, Vickers and Co. They registered a number of designs throughout the period 1847–83, including in 1859 a piano insulator which was made and registered for Thomas Dawkins of Clerkenwell, London. Other items included celery vases, compôtes, dishes, butters, tumblers and flower vases, one of which appeared in the form of a moulded leaf container supported by a dolphin.

The firm concentrated their efforts on the production of table glass in the usual colour range, using the established techniques of cutting, etching, engraving and pressing. They also made retorts and other items for the chemical industry as well as deck and port lights for ships. In all they registered sixteen designs up to 1883. They published a number of catalogues and had a large home and foreign trade.

Joseph Webb, Coalborn Hill Glassworks, Stourbridge

The works were in operation before the middle of the nineteenth century and run by a name well known in Midland glassmaking circles. Webb registered his first design for pressed glass in August 1854. The article shown in the representation was a covered dish, but as is usual the design was applied to a number of different items including a celery vase (see Plate 72).

72 Early celery vase. Note registered design lozenge on the stem. Registered by Joseph Webb of Stourbridge, 3 August 1854.

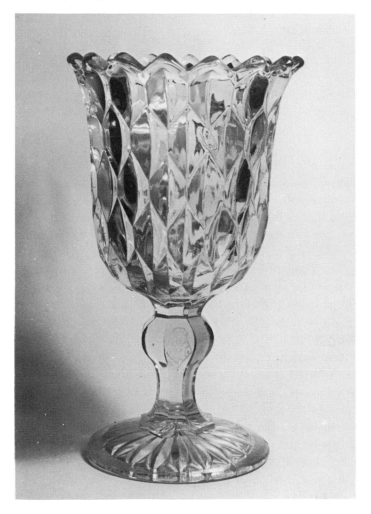

73 Flower trough design registered by Max Sugar on 1 March 1881.

Some time in the 1860s Joseph Webb died and the business was continued by a relative and a partner who traded as 'James Webb and Joseph Hammond, executors of the late Joseph Webb'. They advertised themselves as producing flint and coloured glass 'in all its branches', including table glass, flower stands, vases, troughs, boats and candelabra. Six designs were registered for these types of articles between 1872 and 1874, among which were two flower holders, one in the shape of a swan and the other a boat.

The firm ceased trading in 1888 and their whole stock of moulds was bought by Edward Moore and Co. of South Shields.

Much more research needs to be undertaken into these smaller factories and the many others to which, so far, one has found only fleeting reference. Their names are known to us because they registered a single design, or from a solitary advertisement – many of which were very stereotyped and from which little historical information can be gleaned.

The Lorraine Glass Co. Ltd had a glassworks at Carrhill, Gateshead, where, in 1881, they were producing flint and coloured glass in green, amber, dark and light blue, canary, red and other colours.

74 Very fine purple marbled flower vase in the form of a trumpet. Unmarked, *c.* 1880.

They made free-blown, blow-moulded and pressed glass. The company went into voluntary liquidation in 1885. Also in the north-east was the glasshouse of Matthew Turnbull, at the Cornhill Glassworks, Southwick, Sunderland, who was advertising his pressed table glass in 1887.

In Scotland the only glasshouse specialising in pressed glass, according to a contemporary account, was that of Messrs A. M. Allan and Co. of the Forth Glassworks, Glasgow. In 1884 they were awarded a first-class medal at the Cork Exhibition for their pressed table glass and medicine bottles. They operated three furnaces and were probably founded in the 1870s. They had a network of commercial travellers calling at all the main towns in the United Kingdom, as well as an overseas export trade which was facilitated, as their advertisement points out, by 'regular sailings from the Clyde to Home Coast Ports, the Colonies, India and South American Ports'.

At Tutbury in Staffordshire was the Tutbury Glass Co., founded by a Mr Jackson in the 1830s and continuing for approximately fifty years; it was carried on after his death by his widow. Finally in 1880 the works were sold. Only one design was registered, in 1864, for a suite of table glass with a multiple star pattern.

There is no doubt that the pressed-glass industry was a large employer of labour in the nineteenth century and that there was fierce competition between the many glasshouses who constantly vied with each other in the production of new patterns. Often there was little originality in these 'new patterns', but in order to attract buyers firms had to keep a large range of stock items, many of which may never have seen the light of day. They were left mouldering in some out-of-the-way corner until sold off for a song to some speculative buyer, or destroyed.

CHAPTER 8

DESIGN REGISTRATIONS, TRADE MARKS AND PATENTS

ONE of the interesting aspects of pressed glass is that, in contrast with other types of glass, in many cases the manufacturer can be identified by means of his trade mark or registered design number applied to the article. A complete list of pressed-glass designs registered between 1842 and 1883 is given in Appendix A. This, in conjunction with the chart on page 159, will enable the reader to identify the makers of any article so marked.

Various Acts of Parliament in the late eighteenth century gave protection and sole right of reproduction for up to three months to the designers, printers and proprietors of any design or pattern on linen, cotton, calico and muslin fabrics. An Act of 1839 extended this protection to woollen, silk, hair and other mixed fabrics, as well as increasing the period of protection to twelve months on designs on all textile fabrics not covered by previous Acts. In addition the design, ornamentation, shape or configuration of most other manufactured articles were given twelve months' protection, except in the case of metal articles which were covered for three years. The protection was provisional upon the design being registered, together with the designer's or proprietor's name, with the Registrar of Designs.

However it is the Designs Act of 1842 which really interests us, because under this Act thirteen classes of ornamental designs, including all manufactured goods, were created and designated by Roman numerals. The first four classes were I metal, II wood, III glass and IV ceramics; the other groups mainly concerned fabrics. The period of protection varied from class to class; in the case of glass it was for three years. An Act of the following year extended the protection to cover useful as distinct from ornamental manufactured goods, also for a period of three years.

In 1850 the Act was extended to make possible, for a period of one year, provisional registration of any design that could be registered under the Acts of 1842 and 1843, without affecting its later full registration. Now a period of four years' protection could be obtained.

In order to indicate to other manufacturers and the public at large that a particular design had been registered, the article was usually stamped with a diamond-shaped mark giving details of the class, day, month and year of the original registration, together with the particular bundle of designs in which it was registered. These records are now kept by the Public Record Office at their repository at Kew, and are open to the public. They consist, as far as class III is concerned, of a register running from September 1842 to December 1883 and four volumes of representations. In the register are entered the day, month, year and bundle in which the design was registered together with the design number as entered in the books of representations. The name and address of the firm registering the design are also given but not the name of the actual designer. In some cases a brief description of the type of article is given.

In the volumes of representations are found the actual designs as submitted to the Registry, each of which is given a number. These submissions vary from crude sketches to carefully executed scale drawings, sometimes coloured. In many cases the submission is an actual photograph of the design or article. Henry Greener of Sunderland and William Henry Heppell of Newcastle invariably submitted their designs in this way. The photographs have in some cases faded badly, and in one of W. H. Heppell's designs showing a wheelbarrow the detail is hardly distinguishable.

There are two cycles of diamond-shaped marks – the first running from 1842 to 1867 and the second from 1868 to 1883. The information given in each cycle is the same – it is just the positions on the diamond of the individual items of information that are altered. The registration mark resembles a diamond suspended from a ring, within which is a Roman numeral denoting the class. If you regard the diamond as a clock face, information in the form of a letter or a number appears at twelve o'clock, three o'clock, six o'clock and nine o'clock. For quick identification, if there is a letter at twelve o'clock the registration belongs to the first cycle and that letter gives the year of registration. If there is a number at twelve o'clock the design belongs to the second cycle and the number refers to the day of registration. For a detailed analysis, including a key, see the table on page 159. The reason for the two cycles is the continuing use of letters to represent years. After a period of twenty-six years the repetition of letters would have caused great confusion without re-positioning the letters and numbers. The month codes stay the same, and the year letters are in the same order for each cycle.

There are one or two anomalies worth noting. In 1850 and 1876 VEE is officially used instead of V to denote the year, presumably to avoid confusion with the letter U although in many cases firms actually used V in the mark. In 1857 the letter R was used as the month letter from 1 to 19 September, being a carry-over of the letter from the previous months. There seems to be no obvious reason why this should have occurred, or why in 1860 the letter K should be used for both November and December. Finally from 1 to 6 March 1878 the letter G (instead of W) was used for the month and W (instead of D) for the year (see page 159).

The Patents, Designs and Trade Marks Act of 1883 amalgamated all the various categories of designs, both useful and ornamental, into one continuous series, identified by a number prefixed by 'Registered Number' or 'Rd No.' for short. Starting with Rd No. 1 on 1 January 1884, approximately twenty thousand designs a year were registered. A list of the first numbers registered on 1 January each year up to 1901 is given on page 174 to help pinpoint a registered design to a particular year.

The last Act relating to registered designs that concerns us in this chapter is that of 1907, which extended their protection for a further five years and allowed this period to be extended for yet another five years at the discretion of the Comptroller. This Act may have been somewhat belated if one is to believe a letter published in the *Pottery Gazette* in June 1886, which reads as follows:

Sir,
Have the 'powers that be' any idea to what extent Continental glass people copy English pottery and glass? It is really getting beyond keeping your temper. In fancy glass by Webb, in pressed glass by Sowerby, there is no limit to it, grand glass, common glass, any glass all are copied. One of these days the working men will see it and then it will be handled; then there will be a cry of something like 'England for the English', 'Down with foreign imitations' and so on and shopkeepers who keep such goods will be boycotted. Let the 'powers that be' see it in time and extend the registration laws two or three years longer.

Yours etc.
An Old Manufacturer in Glass

Turning now to Trade Marks, an official pamphlet describes them as 'a means of identification, a symbol (whether word, device, or combination of the two) which a person uses in the course of trade in order that his goods may be readily distinguished by the purchasing public from similar goods of other traders'.

The Trade Marks Registration Act of 1875 first made provision for the registration of trade marks. The Act provided for a register of marks and made registration *prima facie* evidence of the right of the registered proprietor to the exclusive use of the mark in connection with goods of the class for which it was registered and used. It further provided that after five years of registration it should be conclusive proof of such right, provided the proprietor of the mark remained the owner of the goodwill of the business in which it was used. In the 1875 Act no provision was made for the registration of words as such except in association with a mark or device. However the Patents, Design and Trade Marks Act of 1883 remedied this defect.

Trade marks first became officially registrable in January 1876, and it would appear from a contemporary trade journal that manufacturers were slow to avail themselves of this unique and potentially successful means of advertising. Manufacturers were castigated for their dilatory approach and the journal outlined the many advantages that the use of trade marks brought compared to the slight disadvantage of the marginally extra time and cost involved in their application.

Pressed glass lent itself particularly to the use of trade marks, which could be impressed on the opposite side of the article to the pattern, so that they stood out from the plain background and in no way interfered with the pattern. In view of this it is surprising how few firms availed themselves of the opportunity. Only five glass-houses used trade marks to any extent on their wares, and these can be seen in Plate 75. Of these, only two took the trouble to register their marks, as far as I can ascertain. The first was John George Sowerby of the Ellison Flint Glassworks, Gateshead, who registered on 26 January 1876 his famous peacock's head crest for use on all glass articles in opaque colours. The application states that the mark had not been used prior to 13 August 1875, the date on which the Act became law. Although registered for coloured glass only, Sowerby used it in fact on all his pressed glass and also on some of his blown glass, but on the latter the mark is usually indistinct due to lack of pressure. The peacock's head crest is the official family crest of a family called Sowerby, but whether or not it is this particular family I am unable to say. The mark was in fact copied by other firms – possibly some from abroad – during the 1880s, and the firm appealed for information regarding such infringements of their rights and threatening prosecution if the culprits could be found. However there is no record of any such proceedings taking place. The mark was used by the firm as late as the 1930s and I have seen a green glass coronation mug for George VI and Queen Elizabeth bearing this mark.

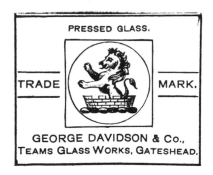

75 Henry Greener's first mark as shown in the register of trade marks at the Patent Office, registered 29 November 1876 and declared not to have been used before August 1875. Also illustrated are the Sowerby and Davidson marks and the second Greener mark (as shown in the *Pottery Gazette* advertisement).

The second registration was by Henry Greener of the Wear Flint Glassworks, Sunderland, who on 29 November 1876 also registered an heraldic crest mark. In this case it was certainly not that of his own family. It took the form of a demi-lion rampant, facing to the left and holding in his dexter (right) paw a five-pointed star. It was registered for use on all kinds of glass and again had not been used before 13 August 1875. It was used by the firm until 1885 when there was a change of ownership. This is the first time that the pre-1885 mark has been recorded in the literature of pressed glass (see Plate 75). Previously it has always been thought that the Greener trade mark was a demi-lion holding a battleaxe in both paws (see Plates 50, 75) but this was the mark introduced by James Jobling after he took over the firm in 1885. The absence of the axe in the earlier mark was previously thought to be the result of poor pressing. The second mark, as far as I am aware, was not registered and first appears in print in the *Pottery Gazette* of 1 March 1886 on a page dealing with trade marks (see Plate 75). It is shown in illustrations as facing to the right but in practice it is usually found facing to the left.

One other firm in the north-east of England used an heraldic crest trade mark and that was George Davidson and Co. of Gateshead. Their mark also takes the form of a demi-lion rampant, this time issuing from a castle turret (referred to heraldically as a mural crown). The lion is facing left (see Plate 75). Again it does not appear to have been taken from a personal grant of arms although a variation of the mark, a lion's head issuing from a mural coronet, is recorded as belonging to an English family of Davidson. The mark was not officially registered and appears for the first time in the pages of the *Pottery Gazette* in April 1883. It was discontinued about 1890 and is probably the rarest of the marks so far mentioned, although the second Greener mark is fairly rare and may also have been discontinued in the 1890s as it disappears from the journal after 1890.

Another trade mark sometimes seen on pressed glass is that used by John Derbyshire of the Regent Flint Glassworks, Salford, Manchester, which takes the form of an anchor superimposed on the initials JD (see Plate 59). At one time this was thought to be the mark of John Davenport who was a glass as well as a porcelain manufacturer and used the anchor mark on his porcelain. However, with the aid of the registered designs register it is now possible to attribute this mark correctly.

The thistle mark in Plate 76 I have found on only two identical

76 Thistle trade mark as seen in the base of a black tripod cauldron sugar basin. Origin unknown, *c.* 1885.

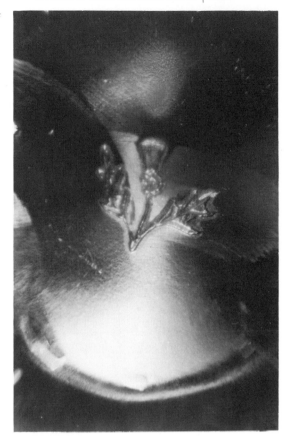

pieces – black tripod cauldrons dating from about 1880 – and it is possibly the mark of one of the Scottish glasshouses, but no further evidence is so far available on this point.

Finally there are a number of trade marks registered by a firm which did not itself make pressed glass but which used glass articles as part of its product – Samuel Clarke of Child's Hill, London. The firm was an old-established one, manufacturer of candles, tapers and night lights and in 1886 they patented their famous Fairy Lamps and Fairy lights for 'ornamentally lighting Drawing and Ball Rooms, Conservatories, Evening Fetes, Table Decorations, etc.'. The firm obtained their pressed-glass containers from various glasshouses – probably the first was Messrs Stuart and Sons, Red Glass Works, Stourbridge. We also know that Thomas Webb and Sons made some of their famous Burmese shades for Clarke. These glass candle containers and shades (see Plate 77) can be found bearing such names as Fairy, Fairy Pyramid, Wee Fairy and Cricklite. All these names were registered, as was the fairy-with-a-wand trade mark which was registered on 1 December 1886.

This completes the list of English glasshouses using trade marks on their products, but a number of American and Continental firms used marks, often in the form of initials, and these will sometimes be found in Britain.

Turning now to the question of patents, many glasshouses in the nineteenth century patented new ideas and inventions for the better production of glassware, and in no branch of the craft were they more numerous than in the field of pressing. The Sowerby Ellison Works alone patented twenty-four new inventions between 1870 and 1900.

It may be helpful to explain first of all the British patent system which had its origins in the Statute of Monopolies of 1623, during the

77 Three-part Clarke's 'Fairy' night-light consisting of inner container, outer base and dome. The base bears the registered 'Fairy' trade mark, c. 1886.

reign of James I. This was enacted in response to a general public outcry against the royal custom of granting trading monopolies such as coal mining, glass manufacture, etc. to royal favourites. Under the statute James agreed to give up the practice except for those concerning new methods of manufacture. One section of the statute, after declaring that all monopolies are illegal, goes on to state

> that any declaration before mentioned shall not extend to any letters patent and grants of privilege, for the term of fourteen years or under, hereafter to be made, of the sole working or making of any manner of new manufactures within the realm to the true and first inventor and inventors of such manufactures; which others at the time of making such Letters Patent and grants shall not use; so as also they be not contrary to the law nor mischievous to the State by raising prices of commodities at home or hurt of trade, or generally inconvenient etc.

The statute benefited the general public in two ways: it no longer deprived them of facilities they had previously enjoyed as was the case with the old system, and by being granted a patent the inventor had to disclose the subject-matter of the patent for the ultimate benefit of the general public on the cessation of the term of his patent.

Following on this statute the British patent system was refined down to its present structure. It is in essence simply a contract between the inventor and the Crown, in which, on condition that the invention is properly defined and fully disclosed so that when the monopoly expires others properly qualified can make use of it, the Crown grants the inventor a monopoly on the use of his invention for a period of years on payment of a fee. The fee was originally payable in full at the time of the grant and so the inventor had to take the risk that his invention would be a commercial success. It is now payable annually by instalments during the term of the monopoly, so that the patent can be abandoned at any time if it is not proving successful. Three things are essential for the grant of a patent. Firstly, the subject-matter must be an article capable of being manufactured or a process in the manufacture of such article. Secondly, the product or process must be a novel one and, thirdly, the invention disclosed must be capable of being utilised.

The patents applying to pressed glass in the nineteenth century were chiefly concerned with new ways of making moulds, pressing mechanisms, finishing processes such as fire-polishing, and the invention of new colours. On 15 September 1871 John George Sowerby was granted patent No. 2433 concerned with 'An improved process of ornamenting pressed glass and an improved apparatus in connection therewith'. This was a method of decorating the outer surface of articles made in pressed glass with designs in glass of a different colour from that of the article. The method is described as:

> First pressing the ornament and while still hot, introducing it into the mould in which the article to be ornamented is to be made, so that in the process of pressing the article the ornamentation becomes incorporated with its outer surface. The mould and plunger used in pressing the ornament have corresponding bevels for the purpose of cutting off all surplus metal from the ornament leaving the design intact.

In 1886 the same firm patented two improvements to the art of fire-polishing the pressed glass after it left the mould. The first was patent No. 4509, dated 31 March, and is concerned with the method of producing the heat in the glory hole where the fire-polishing takes place. By this time oil-fired glory holes were being used, the oil being vapourised by a blast of air across the drip-feed oil pipe. Sowerby's patent consisted of using dry or superheated steam or hot air as the blast. The second invention, No. 6150, dated 6 May, relates to the method of holding the article during fire-polishing. The current method involved the use of a spring clip attached to the end of the punty rod for holding the article, and the invention was to provide asbestos pads and cushions on the jaws and base plate of the clip.

John Sowerby also patented a whole range of new colours in the late 1870s and 80s, including Queen's Ivory (see Plate III), aesthetic green (see Plate I), tortoiseshell, rubine (see Plate IV), etc. This firm was by far the most inventive of all the pressing houses.

In contrast, Henry Greener patented only three inventions, all in the 1870s and relating to pressing jugs and decanters, glass letters and figures and glasses for carriage roof lamps.

George Davidson and Co. were somewhat more inventive, most of their ideas coming from George's son, Thomas. His first patented invention was certainly one of his most successful. Patent No. 2641, accepted on 7 December 1889, is entitled 'Improvements in the Manufacture of Articles of Pressed Glass', and covered the invention of his famous Pearline glass (see Plate VII). Davidson describes it as follows:

According to my invention I manufacture articles such for example as ornamental dishes, vases, jugs, tumblers, and the like of pressed glass in such a manner that at the base they are composed of clear glass or glass of any transparent colour whilst towards the top they gradually become milky and at their upper edge opaque.

This I effect in the following manner:— I take phosphate of lime, arsenic and limespar and mix them well with ordinary materials used for making flint glass, and expose the mixture thus obtained in the usual way in a crucible until ready for working.

The glass is then moulded in the usual way for making pressed glass.

The moulded article which at this stage is transparent I allow to cool for a short time and then expose it on a punty or rod in a strong heat, it then assumes the effect described; the parts most heated being most opaque and the parts not heated so much remaining clear which is regulated by the workman according to the length of time the article is kept in the flame.

The other famous invention of Thomas Davidson's is his well-known flower block or dome (see Plate 44) which he patented in 1910, No. 7830. Many thousands of these are still in existence today, many of them bearing Davidson's patent number, although various modifications were produced once his patent expired. They were made in a range of colours and were either sold separately or *en suite* with a suitable container, usually a bowl. The idea was simply to use the holes in the block to support the stems of the flowers, producing the typical three-dimensional, massed arrangement of the period.

A complete list of the patents of Messrs Sowerby, Greener and Davidson between 1872 and 1910 will be found in Appendix B.

CHAPTER 9

COMMEMORATIVE PIECES

P RESSED glass was ideally suited to the production of cheap commemorative ware. The quality of the finished article, as always with this method of manufacture, depends on the artistic ability of the mouldmaker and the attention to detail of the team attending the press, in order to produce a large output to a consistently high standard. The fine detail possible by this method is especially useful in the reproduction of portraits.

Commemoratives may be grouped under two headings, those representing royal occasions and those depicting famous people, places and events. The first covers such occasions as coronations, jubilees, royal visits, etc., and the second deaths, important new buildings, victory in battle, etc.

The earliest pressed-glass commemoratives are thought to relate to the accession of Queen Victoria, her marriage to Prince Albert of Saxe-Coburg and the birth of her first son, Edward, Prince of Wales – in 1837, 1840 and 1842 respectively. They take the form of a series of five-inch cup plates bearing the name and portrait of Queen Victoria as a young woman, or the name and conjoined portraits of Albert and Victoria, or the three ostrich plumes and motto of the Prince of Wales. The background in each case is a lacy design bearing the floral symbols of England, Scotland and Ireland – roses, thistles and shamrocks (see Plate 78). This floral motif was very popular with pressed-glass designers and occurs frequently throughout the century.

Because of the subjects it was thought at one time that these plates were of English manufacture, but further research seems to indicate that they are the products of the Sandwich Glass Co. of America. This is based on the following observations: (1) Fragments of these plates have been found when excavating the site of the Sandwich glasshouse. (2) The treatment of the design is typical of the Sandwich products of the period. (3) The factory exported glass, in

78 'Prince of Wales plumes' cup plate with national floral emblems. Probably American in origin, *c*. 1842.

particular to the West Indies where there was a large British market. (4) The absence of any evidence relating them to an English manufacturer. (5) The cup plate was a peculiarly American invention which did not catch on in England although some English ceramics factories made cup plates for export to the United States before the advent of American pressed glass.

The cup plate was used originally when tea bowls (cups without handles) were popular, and they were very uncomfortable to hold when full of hot tea. It was then considered perfectly good manners to pour your tea into the saucer, made especially deep for the purpose, to cool. The tea bowl was then placed on the cup plate to prevent damage to polished wood or table linen. The habit continued even after the tea bowls had acquired handles and become teacups.

The first royal commemoratives known to be English relate to Queen Victoria's daughter, Princess Louise, and her husband, the Marquis of Lorne, heir to the Duke of Argyll. They were married in

March 1871 and in June the following year Ker, Webb and Co. registered an ornamental design for a pair of flower vases bearing portraits of the couple but no inscription. In July 1878 the Marquis was created Governor-General of Canada and in November of that year he and the Princess paid a state visit to the Dominion. With astute business acumen and a sharp eye for the Canadian market Henry Greener of the Wear Flint Glassworks, Sunderland, produced a very fine series of designs to be applied to sugar bowls, cream jugs, butter dishes and spooners. The design showed a pair of portrait medallions of the couple, with or without an inscription, commemorating the date of their landing at Halifax, Nova Scotia – 25 November 1878 (see Plates 79 and VIII). The background is filled in

79 The covered butter dish from the series of designs produced by Henry Greener to commemorate the visit of the Marquis and Marchioness of Lorne to Canada in November 1887. The Marquis was Governor-General of Canada, and the Marchioness, Princess Louise, daughter of Queen Victoria. This series is one of the finest designs ever produced in pressed glass. The design was registered on 8 June 1887. (See also Plate VIII and jacket.)

80 Golden Jubilee portrait plate of Queen Victoria by Sowerby Ellison Works, bearing the Sowerby trade mark. The same design with different lettering was used for the Diamond Jubilee. Occasionally the portrait is blocked in gold from the back.

with national floral emblems. The butter dish is particularly fine, bearing both portraits and inscription and having as a knop to the cover a marquess's coronet. The sets were produced in flint glass, opal, malachite, and blue and black majolica. Spooners were short, stubby vases used instead of spoon trays to hold the teaspoons at the tea table before it became the practice to put one in each saucer whether the recipient required it or not.

Towards the end of the century the two jubilees of Queen Victoria caught the imagination of the people and resulted in a spate of souvenirs made from all manner of materials. The Golden Jubilee was in 1887 and the Diamond in 1897, and on both occasions pressed-glass commemoratives were produced. The Sowerby Ellison Works brought out an almost identical plate for the two events, only the wording and date being changed (see Plate 80).

Henry Greener and George Davidson both produced designs for the Golden Jubilee. The former's design for a plate shows a crown in the centre with an orb and sword crossed below, and above, the motto 'God save our Queen'. Around the rim of the plate are the words 'Queen Victoria's Jubilee', separated by two shields, one

81 Brown glass dish commemorating the Golden Jubilee by Greener and Co. Note the second Greener mark under the IC of Victoria. Diam. 5 in (12.5 cm). (See also Plates 50 and 52.)

82 Brown translucent glass plate for the Golden Jubilee produced by George Davidson. No mark, 1887.

bearing the date 1837, the other 1887. The firm also produced a five-inch sweet dish with a similar design but without the motto (see Plate 81). Davidson's contribution is shown in Plate 82 and has in the centre a crown with the pertinent dates above and below and around the side the words 'The Queen's Jubilee'. The following year the same firm brought out a series of articles decorated to commemorate the silver wedding of the Prince and Princess of Wales. These included baskets, bowls, plates, butter dishes, sugars, creams and sweet dishes. They were advertised in a supplement to the *Pottery Gazette*, although unfortunately neither illustration nor description was given. Greener's design for the same event can be seen in Plate 83.

83 Dish commemorating the silver wedding of Edward and Alexandra in 1888. Design registered, Rd. No. 91449, by Greener and Co., 11 January 1888.

For the 1897 Jubilee Thomas Kidd and Co. of Manchester, who specialised in the production of items retailing at one penny each, produced two designs. One was in the form of a hollow bust of the Queen, bearing a name but no date (see Plate 84) and the other was a five-inch plate with a portrait of the Queen in the centre, and above, the words 'Queen Victoria – England's Greatest Queen' and below, 'Fairest and Noblest the World has ever seen'. Around the rim was a circle of stylised flowers with a beaded border. Both items were illustrated in the firm's advertisement (see Plate 71).

There does not appear to have been any design produced by the English houses for that most shattering and far-reaching of all Victorian royal events, the death of Prince Albert in 1861. A small cup plate is known, bearing a portrait and the word 'Albert' but no date. It would appear to be contemporary with those mentioned at the beginning of this chapter and almost certainly of American origin.

84 Opaque black bust of Queen Victoria produced by Thomas Kidd, Manchester, for the Diamond Jubilee of 1897. (See also Plate 71.)

On 10 November 1870 Henry Greener registered a design for a sugar basin with the inscription around the top 'Friedrich Wilhelm', separated by Maltese crosses. This could refer to Frederick William, Crown Prince of Prussia and later Imperial Prince of Germany who married Princess Victoria, eldest daughter of the Queen, in 1858, or to his son Frederick William, born in 1859. It is likely to refer to the former, who was involved in the outbreak of the Franco–Prussian War in 1870.

In the twentieth century pressed items were produced for each coronation, including that of Edward V I I I which did not take place.

85 Design for the Diamond Jubilee by Greener and Co. No mark, 1897.

The second group of commemoratives, and by far the larger, covers people, places and events, and records particularly the deaths of eminent men of the time together with certain highlights in their lives. Local heroes and events were also remembered by the glasshouses. The earliest of these was the opening of the new High Level Bridge over the river Tyne at Newcastle upon Tyne on 16 January 1850, commemorated in a very fine mug (see Plate 86) depicting the bridge with a railway locomotive passing over it. Around the top are the words 'High level bridge, Newcastle on Tyne', and below, between the arches, 'Commenced April 24, 1846' and 'Opened January 16, 1850'. It is not possible at present to attribute it to a particular manufacturer, but as the south end of the bridge was only a short distance from Pipewellgate, Gateshead, where a number of glasshouses were situated including the New Stourbridge Works of John Sowerby, it is reasonable to suppose that one of these was responsible.

Particularly prominent in the production of commemoratives in the 1870s and 1880s was the firm of Henry Greener and Co., Sunderland. In 1869 they produced two designs. One, in the nature of an acclaim for the new Prime Minister bears the inscription 'Gladstone for the Million' (see Plate 46). The second design, registered in December, relates to the achievements of the Anglo-American philanthropist George Peabody (1795–1869) on 4 December. Born in Massachusetts of poor parents he made his own way in the world. Having established himself in a wholesale dry goods business with branches in various parts of the United States, he came to England in connection with that business in 1827. Ten years later he took up permanent residence in England and, severing his ties with the

86 Mug commemorating the building and opening of the High Level Bridge across the river Tyne. A railway train can be seen crossing the bridge, and the mug bears the inscriptions 'Commenced April 24 1846' and 'Opened January 16 1850'. No mark, c. 1850.

American firm, he began business in London as a merchant banker. He was a great benefactor on both sides of the Atlantic. It is as a supporter of education and a builder of better housing for the working classes that he is chiefly remembered. In all he gave a total of £500,000 to the City of London, from which the famous Peabody Buildings – model dwellings for the poor – were developed. The first block was opened in Spitalfields in 1864 and others followed in Chelsea, Bermondsey, Islington and Shadwell. Many public honours were offered to him (which he declined), including a baronetcy and the Order of the Bath from Queen Victoria. He did, however, accept an address from the working men of London. After his death, his body lay in state for a month at Westminster Abbey before being taken to America for burial in his home town of Danvers.

The design, which is seen to best advantage on a flat plate, shows, in the centre, a crown within a heart – presumably representing his charity – and radiating outwards a series of concentric lines with three circles of stars representing the stars and stripes of America. His name appears in large letters around the edge (see Plate 87). This design is also found on dishes, cups, saucers, sugar bowls, etc.

On 28 July 1885 the death occurred of another well-known philanthropist of his day, Sir Moses Montefiore, at the ripe old age of

87 Plate commemorating the achievements of the American philanthropist George Peabody, who died on 4 December 1869. He was a great benefactor to the poor of London. The design, which can be found on many other articles, was registered by Henry Greener, 31 July 1869.

88 Fine portrait plate commemorating the Jewish philanthropist Sir Moses Montefiore who died on 28 July 1885, aged 100 years. Unmarked, *c.* 1885.

a hundred. He came from a long line of internationally famous Jewish families, his grandfather emigrating to London in the mid-eighteenth century. Montefiore spent his early adult life in mercantile banking, eventually acquiring the right to act as a broker on the London Stock Exchange where the number of Jewish brokers was then limited to twelve. He soon amassed a fortune and in 1824, aged thirty-nine, he retired from business and devoted the rest of his life to the service of the Jewish race at home and abroad. In 1837 he became Sheriff of London and was knighted by Queen Victoria on the occasion of her visit to the Guildhall. His death was commemorated on a portrait plate (see Plate 88), which unfortunately bears no mark of origin.

International exhibitions of ceramics and glass often produced commemorative pieces, one of the more unusual being the design by

89 A fine design for the Glasgow Exhibition of 1888. Although unmarked, the cut-glass effects in the centre are reminiscent of the Greener design in Plate 55, and this plate may well be one of their products.

Greener and Co. for the Paris Exhibition of 1889, which was a model of the Eiffel Tower in the form of a candlestick. This is particularly appropriate since it commemorates both the Exhibition and the erection of the Tower itself which was produced specially for the Exhibition.

The Glasgow International Exhibition of 1888 was commemorated by a plate (see Plate 89). This is a fine example, using the potential of the pressing method to advantage. It is a mixture of lacy design and imitation cut glass with the words 'Glasgow May 1888 International Exhibition', and, in a diagonal band across the plate, the motto 'Let Glasgow Flourish'. Some pretty thistle decoration completes the design.

It is interesting that a contemporary report of the Exhibition (*Pottery Gazette*, 1 September 1888) does not seem very enamoured of the show as a whole and castigates manufacturers for the lack of good-quality pressed glass: 'What we seem to miss in this Exhibition is the common pressed glass of the North, for the few specimens of pressed glass certainly only misrepresent the trade.'

In July 1874 John Derbyshire of the Regent Flint Glassworks, Manchester, registered a design for a paperweight in the shape of a recumbent lion identical to the ones at the base of Nelson's Column in Trafalgar Square (see Plate 60). These lions had been designed by the great Victorian animal painter, Sir Edwin Landseer RA, and since Landseer had died the previous year it is possible that the paperweights were meant to commemorate, if not his death, then his achievements in life. This firm produced from time to time a number of animal subjects based on Landseer's works, including dogs (see Plate 61).

Statesmen were always good subjects for the pressed glass designers, as shown by the glass busts of Gladstone and Disraeli (see Plate 90); they have a frosted finish and bear no indication as to their origin. They date from the 1880s when the two men were at the height of their careers and much in the public eye. Similar busts

90 A pair of frosted glass busts of Gladstone and Disraeli. Unmarked, they probably date from the 1880s.

of the Queen and Prince Albert were produced in the 1840s by the Birmingham firm of F. & C. Osler. Disraeli, the Earl of Beaconsfield, was also the subject of a design produced and registered by Henry Greener, recording the statesman's success at the Congress of Berlin in 1878. The design is seen most frequently on a sugar basin and cream jug (see Plate 91); it has a portrait medallion on one side and an inscription on the other, which reads 'Earl Beaconsfield the Hero of the Congress, Berlin, July 1878' – both pieces of decoration are surrounded by a wreath of laurel leaves. The space between is filled with the floral emblems of England, Scotland and Ireland. The small cream jug bears only the portrait medallion without the inscription.

As well as great national figures local heroes were also honoured in pressed glass. A good example is the mug – again produced by

91 Sugar basin and cream jug in milk-white glass by Henry Greener commemorating Lord Beaconsfield's (Disraeli's) success at the Congress of Berlin in 1878. Design registered 31 August 1878. The basin bears the first Greener mark and the design lozenge.

92 Bottle-green jockey boot with inscriptions commemorating Lord Rosebery's Derby winner, Ladas, in 1894. Unmarked. (The boot also exists without the inscriptions.)

Greener – recording the two occasions when the World Rowing Championship, held on the river Tyne, was won by a local resident, Edward Hanlon. In 1880 he beat a man called Tuckett and in 1882 he beat Boyd of Middlesbrough. The design, which was registered and shows a man in a rowing boat with an appropriate inscription, served both occasions, only the inscription being altered. Edward Hanlon was a native of Canada who lived in Newcastle where rowing was a very popular sport on the Tyne in the nineteenth century. In later life he returned to Canada where he died in Toronto in 1908.

Moulds were expensive things to produce, and the use of one to serve two or more purposes, as above, was not infrequent. It was made possible by designing the moulds with several side pieces bearing different inscriptions – to be inserted as required. Another example is seen in Plate 92. The inscription commemorates the winning of the Derby in 1894 by Lord Rosebery's horse, Ladas. Around the top of the boot are the words, 'M. Dawson, Trainer, J.

93 A model of Cleopatra's Needle in milk-white glass. Unmarked, *c.* 1878.

Watts, Jockey', and across the front, 'Lord Rosebery's Ladas, Winner of Derby, 1894'.

In September 1878 the obelisk known as Cleopatra's Needle was put in position on the Thames Embankment. It was originally set up as one of a pair at Heliopolis about 1500 BC. They were of rose-red Syrene granite, covered with hieroglyphics, and estimated to weigh over two hundred tons. The setting-up of one by the banks of the Thames caused a great stir at the time and resulted in a number of commemorative items including at least two in glass. One (see Plate 93) is a simple model of the obelisk covered in hieroglyphics and of unknown origin. The other, which is also a model of the Needle, was intended for use as a jar for pomade or other substance and was a design registered by the firm of G. V. de Luca, London, on 13 October 1877.

Much of Victoria's reign was taken up with Empire-building and colonial wars. Many of the events were the subjects of glass and ceramic mementoes. One example, recording the death of General Gordon at the siege of Khartoum in 1885, is in the form of a brown glass ink bottle (see Plate 94). Gordon had earned the nickname 'Chinese Gordon' because of his many military exploits in China in the 1860s. The design bears a portrait of Gordon wearing a fez and on either side of the portrait, which is encircled with laurel leaves, are shields, one with the inscription 'Born 23rd Jan 1833', the other 'Died at Khartoum 26th Jan 1885'. Around the top are the words 'Chinese Gordon' and 'Ink Bottle'.

Finally in this chapter, although not strictly commemorative, reference should be made to a number of pieces depicting English

94 Brown glass inkwell commemorating the death of General Gordon at Khartoum, 26 January 1885.

95 A fine model of the English fictional character John Bull, complete with dog, cudgel and copy of *The Times*. Unmarked, *c.* 1875.

popular and allegorical figures. John Derbyshire of the Regent Flint Glassworks, Manchester, produced a number of these including Britannia and Punch and Judy. In November 1874 he registered a design for the seated figure of Britannia, and in May 1876 another design for a tobacco box with the figure of Britannia on the lid and four panels on the body bearing figures representing the four continents – Europe, Asia, Africa and America. The box is possibly meant to symbolise the British Empire.

Plate 63 shows the seated figure of Judy with a cat, one of a pair of Punch and Judy figures also produced by Derbyshire in both clear and frosted glass. These well-loved figures of English seaside shows were derived from characters in the Italian *commedia dell'arte*. Originally played by live actors, the characters later assumed the glove puppet form of popular Victorian entertainment.

Completing this group is the figure of John Bull (see Plate 95). This fine example of the mouldmaker's art, although unmarked, probably came from the same glasshouse, since there are similarities in the shape of the bases. John Bull epitomises all that was thought to be typical of the English character. He first appeared in a series of pamphlets issued by John Arbuthnot in 1712 which were designed to represent in humorous allegory the cessation of war with France. John Bull was described as honest but quarrelsome, his temper depending on the weather; he understood business, and was fond of drinking and the society of his friends. The model shows him sitting on a bale of wool, with his bulldog carrying a copy of *The Times* in his mouth. He is wearing a waistcoat and tailcoat with a fob hanging from his breeches pocket and a monocle on a string around his neck. In his hand he holds a cudgel.

96 An inexpensive Victorian Christmas gift, *c.* 1885, typical of designs in the last quarter of the 19th century. Although unmarked, the border is typical of designs produced by both Davidson and Greener (see Plates 82 and 89).

This review of pressed-glass commemoratives is by no means exhaustive, nor could it be since much remains to be recorded about these interesting vignettes of Victorian life. It will be noted that with an eye to the commercial viability of their products the glasshouses chose, on the whole, to commemorate people and events that would appeal to the great mass of their customers who were in the lower half of the social scale and who might be expected to have a particular interest in philanthropists and national heroes of the day.

CHAPTER 10

COLLECTING
PRESS-MOULDED GLASS

WHEN forming any collection three things are required – time, knowledge and money. The more one has of one the less one needs of the others. With a lot of knowledge and plenty of time to search, a reasonable collection of pressed glass can be acquired for a very modest outlay. On the other hand a wealthy individual can pay someone to do the collecting, in which case you require neither time nor knowledge, only money. There is no doubt, however, that the real thrill in collecting comes in finding bargains.

In any type of collecting the cardinal rule is, whenever possible always buy perfect specimens. This is particularly important with glass because repairs, especially to clear glass, are difficult and never very satisfactory. In the beginning it is permissible to buy damaged material in order to have an example of a particular colour or shape, but make sure that the price is adjusted accordingly and replace the piece as soon as possible with a perfect example. The true value of a damaged piece only really becomes apparent when one tries to sell it again. Chips reduce the price considerably, while cracks of any magnitude render the piece practically worthless from a commercial point of view.

If your collecting has to be done on a strict budget, try to set aside a fixed sum each week or month, so that you build up a small amount of capital. There is nothing more frustrating than discovering a desirable piece at the right price and finding out that you cannot afford to lay out £10 or £15 that month. At the present time (1979) prices vary considerably from under £1 for good examples of clear flint glass kitchen articles to £70 or £80 for rare coloured or commemorative items, and prices will almost certainly continue to rise.

The more time you can make available to search antique shops, junk shops and salerooms on a regular basis, the better. It is by being in the right place at the right time that bargains are acquired.

The third ingredient is knowledge. Time spent in its acquisition is always well spent and will repay you handsomely in terms of your collection. It will enable you to spot the rare and unusual at a glance, to discover trade marks and registration marks missed by others and to distinguish originals from reproductions. Illustrations and information can be found in many general books on glass and antiques (see the Bibliography at the end of this book). A valuable primary source of material is the *Pottery Gazette and Glass Trades Journal*, usually referred to as the *Pottery Gazette*, which began publication in the early 1870s and continued into the present century. It was published in weekly parts and bound quarterly volumes are available for reference at the Victoria and Albert Museum Library and the National Newspaper and Periodical Library, Colindale, London NW9. Local librarians will be able to advise you if there is a series held nearer your home. To anyone interested in Victorian pottery, porcelain or glass they make fascinating reading.

A small pocket notebook is useful for recording prices and other details of items not bought, for future reference. If you own a good-quality single lens reflex camera it can be put to good use. Most dealers, once you get to know them, are willing to let you photograph pieces which you are not able, or do not wish, to buy, although they are liable to become disenchanted if you avail yourself too often of the facility without buying anything. A good relationship with dealers is essential if you want desirable pieces put on one side in the back room until you call. This is another reason for making regular, frequent visits, particularly if you are not the only customer collecting pressed glass.

'Small is beautiful' is a current catchphrase and it can be very true of a collection. Unless you are setting out to produce a national reference collection, a small collection of top quality pieces chosen for their rarity and interest is more pleasing and financially rewarding then a large collection of miscellaneous junk which looks as though the only thought behind it was how little could be spent on each piece.

The following factors should be taken into account when assessing the value of a piece, although some of them obviously rely on personal taste: condition, colour, shape, utility, association and fashion. Condition we have already dealt with as regards damage, but some evidence of wear, particularly on the foot rim of an article, can be a useful guide to authenticity – but more about this later. Colour can be a matter of personal choice but some colours occur less frequently than others and so the price will be higher. Other things being equal, a colourless piece of flint glass will command the lowest price, followed by black or white (milk glass) pieces, then purple marbled colours. Pale blue, blue and white marbled, and green and white marbled are next, and finally come the rare colours – aesthetic green (Sowerby: see Plate I), yellow (see Plate I), brown Pearline (see Plate VII), lilac and ruby (rubine, Sowerby: see plate IV). I have omitted from this list the ubiquitous iridescent glass produced at the end of the century and now known by the American name of carnival glass. This is in a class on its own and is very much a matter of personal taste. Prices for this type of glass are affected by the demand from the United States.

Shape is another matter of personal taste, although on the whole animal shapes and figures, either functional or decorative, command a greater appeal and therefore a higher price than the more conventional shapes. Utility – whether or not a piece can be put to some useful purpose, whether or nor it is the one for which it was originally intended – will certainly affect the price. Not everyone who buys pressed glass is a collector – some will buy the odd piece because they find it attractive and it will serve some useful purpose.

Association – here one includes such items as commemorative pieces, associated with the death of someone or some great event – will make the price higher because the market is much greater. Not only are we in the field of pressed-glass collectors, but we are also in the province of general commemorative collectors who form a far larger body at the present time. Association can apply to a piece which has belonged to someone important or come from a famous collection, which will also enhance its value. Under this heading too we must include trade marks and registered design numbers, since they enable us to associate the piece with its manufacturer. Again pieces bearing these marks will have a greatly increased value over similar pieces without such marks.

Fashions come and go almost monthly and some of them can be very deplorable, such as drilling holes in the bases of ceramic or glass containers to take a flex when converting them to table lamps. However prices of certain things can suddenly rocket because they have become fashionable. Unfortunately for us if we have paid the higher price, they can equally suddenly descend once the fashion has changed.

In the beginning it is best to aim at a broad, representative collection until a personal preference for a particular period or factory begins to emerge. You may decide to collect only commemorative pieces, or coloured pieces, or those of a particular style. The choice is fairly wide but the more specialised the collection the more you are likely to have to pay for individual items, unless you can find some obscure aspect on the subject to specialise in, which appeals to you but is not currently popular.

Personal appeal is very important to collecting. The majority of the pieces you buy should always have a personal attraction for you. Occasionally it is necessary to acquire an example, for the sake of completing a set, which you find not particularly attractive. My personal aversion is orange carnival glass – nevertheless my collection contains one or two pieces because it has a significant place in the story of pressed glass.

Having acquired the beginnings of a collection, next comes the question of cataloguing and displaying it. Detailed records should be kept of all pieces, giving date and place purchased, price paid, and all the details of the piece you have been able to discover, including any references to it or illustrations of it, in the literature. It is a good idea to collect dealers' trade cards, particularly those a long way from home, since a telephone call at a later date can save a wasted journey. The records may be kept in a notebook, either fixed or loose leaf, or in a five by three-inch card system for easy reference. Each piece should be given a reference number which can be written on the base with a Rotring pen and protected by a thin coat of clear nail varnish. Write this number into the catalogue. This becomes more important as the collection grows and it becomes impossible to remember every individual piece with its details.

Displaying glass, particularly clear flint glass, can be a problem. Background colour and lighting are very important. For ease of maintenance, general appearance and safety the collection is best housed in a closed cabinet. Items displayed on open surfaces collect dust, can be knocked over and even used as ashtrays by thoughtless visitors. Free-standing china and glass display cabinets are now extremely expensive but are a good investment and will always find a ready market should you wish to dispose of them later. For the do-it-yourself enthusiast built-in units are the answer. The recesses either side of a chimney breast are a good location, or you can fill the whole length of a room wall. In either case the back and sides of the unit are provided; all that you require are shelving and a front. The front can most easily be made using a sliding door type of double-glazing system. Shelving should be adjustable and of clear plate glass, which makes uniform lighting easier. Long lengths of neon striplighting give the best all-over effect and may be placed at the top and bottom or on either side. Experiment with both positions before final fixing.

If a mixture of coloured and clear glass is to be displayed a neutral colour background is best – off-white, grey or beige – which can be made of unpatterned wallpaper or materials of various types including velvet, according to your taste and pocket. I find a watered silk effect particularly attractive. A well-arranged and illuminated display cabinet can be an asset to a room and give useful background lighting.

A photographic record of the collection can be useful in many ways. If pieces are stolen they are more easily identifiable. Colour prints can provide a simple method of carrying your collection with you should you wish to compare pieces in a shop or illustrate some point to a dealer or fellow collector. Colour slides can be useful if at any time you are asked to give a talk about your collection, which is quite likely to happen once your interest becomes known. As with displaying, photographs should be taken against a neutral background to avoid visual distractions, and grey velvet gives good results. Lighting the object to bring out details of the design without producing objectionable shadows is also important, and may require some experiment.

Let us now move to the question of authenticity. One of the questions you should always ask yourself when buying a piece of pressed glass is: Is it right – is it what it appears to be or is it a contemporary copy, later reproduction or an altered piece? We know from Chapter 3 that Sowerby's products at least were being copied at the time, using the firm's trade mark. These can sometimes be identified by poor workmanship and finishing since genuine Sowerby pieces are finished to a high standard. The quality of the metal can also be a useful guide although it must be admitted that a great deal of experience is necessary to spot copies of this type. More easy to detect are the modern reproductions of Victorian pieces. In the last few years an interest in pressed glass has arisen, particularly in America, and some firms have started reproducing items, using the original moulds if available. Brass and gunmetal moulds have a long life and many are still in existence. In all cases where old moulds are used these reproductions will bear any trade marks or registered design numbers that were on the original. In some cases the reproductions are being produced by the same firm who made the originals. There is nothing illegal about pieces bearing Victorian registration marks being made today, since all the mark indicates is that the design was registered on a certain date. Protection of the design will long since have expired.

As far as English pressed glass is concerned the commonest reproductions met with are sugar bowls and cream jugs made in the blue Pearline glass patented by Davidson. These can usually be spotted by their pristine condition and frequent appearance. One usually finds after a salesman has been round that many of the antique shops in the district have got a Pearline sugar and cream set in the window and that, even if purchased, another set will take its place the following day. Examination of the foot rim usually reveals complete absence of wear, which should make one suspicious. Sometimes pieces are artificially aged by rubbing the foot rim on an abrasive surface such as a brick wall or stone floor. However, the matt appearance of genuine wear is not easy to simulate, and all too often linear or curved striations appear on the foot rim, showing that the piece has been rubbed up and down in a straight line or in circles.

Reproductions of old pressed glass are also being produced on the Continent and in America. In some instances there is no intent to deceive and such pieces often bear the name of their country of origin, showing them to have been made after 1891. The reason for this is an Act introduced into the United States Legislature in 1891 called the McKinley Tariff Act, which among other things stipulated that goods imported into the United States should bear the name of their country of origin. In the case of pressed glass the only way this could be done was to have the name cut into the mould, so all the pieces bear the name – not just those exported to America. Pieces marked 'Czechoslovakia' and 'France' are most frequently found, although apart from the style it is not possible to tell exactly when, after 1891, the piece was made.

In America, pressed glass is still big business for both decorative and utilitarian purposes and many of the older firms are reproducing their earlier items from the original moulds. One such company is the Imperial Glass Co., whose products usually bear the monogram IG.

The problem must be seen in perspective. The majority of English nineteenth-century pressed glass is not being reproduced at the present time. Moreover the manufacture of new moulds would be an extremely costly venture and would not be justified unless the value of the original items rose to such a height as to make reproductions a commercially viable proposition.

One final thing should be remembered – pieces can be altered to conceal previous damage. An example of this can be seen in Plate VI. The original Davidson spill holder is shown next to a piece that has been ground down to resemble a salt cellar. It has subsequently been polished to hide the evidence, but the cut-off pattern gives the game away. Repairs are also possible on opaque coloured glass; they are rather more difficult to detect than on clear flint glass. If an item appears cheap for what it is, always examine it carefully for evidence of damage and possibly repair. If you are in any doubt as to condition or age it is always worth while asking the dealer a direct question. Few will tell a direct lie and most will give an honest opinion to the best of their knowledge. If you do not ask you will not always be told.

REGISTERED DESIGNS

(a) 1842 to 1867

1 January 1843

	Years		Months	
	1842 — X	1855 — E	January	— C
	1843 — H	1856 — L	February	— G
	1844 — C	1857 — K	March	— W
	1845 — A	1858 — B	April	— H
	1846 — I	1859 — M	May	— E
	1847 — F	1860 — Z	June	— M
	1848 — U	1861 — R	July	— I
	1849 — S	1862 — O	August	— R
	1850 — V	1863 — G	September	— D
	1851 — P	1864 — N	October	— B
	1852 — D	1865 — W	November	— K
	1853 — Y	1866 — Q	December	— A
	1854 — J	1867 — T		

(R may be found as the month mark for 1–19 September 1857, and K for December 1860.)

(b) 1868 to 1883

1st January 1869

Years		Months	
1868 — X	1876 — V	January	— C
1869 — H	1877 — P	February	— G
1870 — C	1878 — D	March	— W
1871 — A	1879 — Y	April	— H
1872 — I	1880 — J	May	— E
1873 — F	1881 — E	June	— M
1874 — U	1882 — L	July	— I
1875 — S	1883 — K	August	— R
		September	— D
		October	— B
		November	— K
		December	— A

(For 1–6 March 1878, G was used for the month and W for the year.)

A List of All Registered Designs in Pressed Glass, 1842–1883

Year	Month	Day	Bundle	Firm Registering the Design
1847	November	27	2	Percival and Yates, Manchester
1848	February	11	2	Percival and Yates, Manchester
	March	18	4	Jonas Defries, Houndsditch, London
1849	July	18	4	Daniel Wilkinson, Manchester
1850	February	6	9	Henry Trinder, Watling St, London
	February	15	8	George Sherwood and Co., St Helens, Lancashire
	May	23	4	George Sherwood and Co., St Helens, Lancashire
	July	24	7	George Green, Broad Street, Birmingham
1853	June	23	2	Joseph Webb, Stourbridge
	December	17	1	Joseph Webb, Stourbridge
1854	January	14	3	Benjamin Richardson, Stourbridge
	June	15	2	Joseph Webb, Stourbridge
	August	3	1	Joseph Webb, Stourbridge
	October	23	6	Benjamin Richardson, Stourbridge
	November	18	4	Joseph Webb, Stourbridge
1857	March	21	3	Joseph Webb, Stourbridge
1858	August	28	2	Joseph Webb, Stourbridge
	December	21	6	Angus and Greener, Sunderland
1859	July	8	2	Percival, Yates and Vickers, Manchester
1861	June	27	1	Edward Moore and Co., South Shields
	June	29	4	Edward Moore and Co., South Shields
	December	19	4	David Jacobs, Finsbury Square London
1862	October	1	3	Elizer Edwards, Birmingham
1863	July	9	8	Elizer Edwards, Birmingham

1864	January	11	11	Tutbury Glass Co., Tutbury, Staffordshire
	June	14	4	James Derbyshire and Bro., Manchester
	August	27	4	Molineaux and Webb, Manchester
	November	2	4	James Derbyshire and Bro., Manchester
	December	10	7	James Derbyshire and Bro., Manchester
	December	22	6	Molineaux and Webb, Manchester
1865	March	21	6	Percival, Yates and Vickers, Manchester
	May	12	6	Molineaux and Webb, Manchester
	May	16	4	James Derbyshire and Bro., Manchester
	May	29	8	Molineaux and Webb, Manchester
	August	15	4	James Derbyshire and Bro., Manchester
	August	25	6	James Derbyshire and Bro., Manchester
	September	12	2	James Derbyshire and Bro., Manchester
	October	4	4	Molineaux, Webb and Co., Manchester
	October	31	8	Molineaux, Webb and Co., Manchester
	November	23	9	David Jacobs, Finsbury Square, London
	December	14	5	James Derbyshire and Bro., Manchester
	December	14	6	James Couper and Sons, Glasgow
1866	January	18	6	Molineaux, Webb and Co., Manchester
	January	20	2	Molineaux, Webb and Co., Manchester

Year	Month	Day	Bundle	Firm Registering the Design
	January	30	7	Molineaux, Webb and Co., Manchester
	February	15	2	Molineaux, Webb and Co., Manchester
	May	8	2	Elizer Edwards, Birmingham
	May	10	4	McDermott, Conolly and Co., Pipewellgate, Gateshead
	May	24	1	Angus and Greener, Sunderland
	June	16	4	James Derbyshire and Bro., Manchester
	August	25	6	Angus and Greener, Sunderland
1867	January	26	4	Angus and Greener, Sunderland
	February	25	5	James Derbyshire and Bro., Manchester
	June	24	3	Molineaux, Webb and Co., Manchester
	June	26	8	Angus and Greener, Sunderland
	August	10	3	Molineaux, Webb and Co., Manchester
	August	26	5	Molineaux, Webb and Co., Manchester
	September	10	4	Molineaux, Webb and Co., Manchester
	October	18	4	Robinson and Boulton, Orford Lane, Warrington
	November	26	9	Angus and Greener, Sunderland
1868	January	13	1	Molineaux, Webb and Co., Manchester
	January	31	9	Molineaux, Webb and Co., Manchester
	January	31	9	Molineaux, Webb and Co., Manchester
	February	8	4	Molineaux, Webb and Co., Manchester
	March	5	11	Edward Moore and Co., South Shields
	April	1	7	Angus and Greener, Sunderland

	May	4	6	Angus and Greener, Sunderland
	May	29	11	James Derbyshire and Bro., Manchester
	July	11	4	Molineaux, Webb and Co., Manchester
	August	20	6	Molineaux, Webb and Co., Manchester
	December	21	4	Percival, Vickers and Co., Manchester
1869	February	1	12	Molineaux, Webb and Co., Manchester
	March	27	1	Molineaux, Webb and Co., Manchester
	April	13	7	James Derbyshire and Bro., Manchester
	April	20	9	Angus and Greener, Sunderland
	July	31	8	Henry Greener, Sunderland
	August	12	8	Henry Greener, Sunderland
	December	7	7	Henry Greener, Sunderland
1870	January	3	3	Molineaux, Webb and Co., Manchester
	January	14	11	Henry Greener, Sunderland
	February	22	4	Molineaux, Webb and Co., Manchester
	April	2	4	Molineaux, Webb and Co., Manchester
	May	26	6	Molineaux, Webb and Co., Manchester
	June	21	3	J. J. and T. Derbyshire, Manchester
	July	6	2	Molineaux, Webb and Co., Manchester
	August	1	1	Percival, Vickers and Co., Manchester
	November	18	2	Molineaux, Webb and Co., Manchester
1871	January	17	7	Molineaux, Webb and Co., Manchester

Year	Month	Day	Bundle	Firm Registering the Design
	January	24	3	Molineaux, Webb and Co., Manchester
	March	2	8	Henry Greener, Sunderland
	March	15	9	J. J. and T. Derbyshire, Manchester
	April	29	9	Edward Bolton, Warrington, Lancashire
	May	25	12	John Henry Wood, Portman Square, London
	October	3	4	Burtles, Tate and Co., Manchester
1872	February	2	1	Sowerby Ellison Glassworks, Gateshead
	February	12	1	Woodhall, Keen and Woodhall, Birmingham
	February	12	6	Sowerby Ellison Glassworks, Gateshead
	February	22	6	Hodgetts, Richardson and Son, Stourbridge
	February	29	5	Sowerby Ellison Glassworks, Gateshead
	March	25	5	J. J. and T. Derbyshire, Manchester
	May	11	9	J. J. and T. Derbyshire, Manchester
	June	13	3	Ker, Webb and Co., Manchester
	June	21	6	J. Webb and J. Hammond, Stourbridge
	November	6	11	J. J. and T. Derbyshire, Manchester
	November	7	7	Sowerby Ellison Glassworks, Gateshead
	December	10	7	Henry Greener, Sunderland
	December	11	4	J. J. and T. Derbyshire, Manchester
	December	14	8	J. J. and T. Derbyshire, Manchester

	December 19	3	J. Webb and J. Hammond, Stourbridge
1873	January 3	4	J. Webb and J. Hammond, Stourbridge
	February 12	1	Daniel Pearce, Hammersmith, London
	April 16	4	J. Webb and J. Hammond, Stourbridge
	May 27	6	Ker, Webb and Co., Manchester
	June 20	13	Sowerby Ellison Glassworks, Gateshead
	July 31	5	Sowerby Ellison Glassworks, Gateshead
	August 8	7	John Derbyshire, Salford, Manchester
	September 2	9	John Derbyshire, Salford, Manchester
	December 10	11	J. Webb and J. Hammond, Stourbridge
1874	January 6	6	John Derbyshire, Salford, Manchester
	January 15	6	Sowerby Ellison Glassworks, Gateshead
	February 3	5	John Derbyshire, Salford, Manchester
	February 14	10	Molineaux, Webb and Co., Manchester
	April 22	8	Sowerby Ellison Glassworks, Gateshead
	May 12	6	John Derbyshire, Salford, Manchester
	May 29	2	John Hanbury, Birmingham
	June 1	8	Sowerby Ellison Glassworks, Gateshead
	June 15	1	J. Webb and J. Hammond, Stourbridge

Year	Month	Day	Bundle	Firm Registering the Design
	July	3	4	John Derbyshire, Salford, Manchester
	July	29	8	Percival, Vickers and Co., Manchester
	August	17	5	Sowerby Ellison Glassworks, Gateshead
	August	26	5	William Henry Heppell, Newcastle
	September	10	6	Sowerby Ellison Glassworks, Gateshead
	September	11	5	John Derbyshire, Salford, Manchester
	October	28	7	Edward Bolton, Warrington
	November	26	5	John Derbyshire, Salford, Manchester
	December	21	4	J. Webb and J. Hammond, Stourbridge
1875	January	1	2	Sowerby Ellison Glassworks, Gateshead
	February	12	9	Molineaux, Webb and Co., Manchester
	February	26	4	Molineaux, Webb and Co., Manchester
	March	30	4	John Short Downing, Birmingham
	April	19	5	Sowerby Ellison Glassworks, Gateshead
	June	5	9	Sowerby Ellison Glassworks, Gateshead
	July	26	3	Molineaux, Webb and Co., Manchester
	August	5	8	John Derbyshire, Salford, Manchester
	September	10	6	Sowerby Ellison Glassworks, Gateshead
	October	16	10	Molineaux, Webb and Co., Manchester

	October	23	3	William Henry Heppell, Newcastle
	October	28	4	Sowerby Ellison Glassworks, Gateshead
	November 13	4	William Henry Heppell, Newcastle
	December	6	7	John Derbyshire and Co., Manchester
	December 17	16	Sowerby Ellison Glassworks, Gateshead
1876	February	25	8	John Ford, Edinburgh
	March	6	3	Sowerby Ellison Glassworks, Gateshead
	March	9	7	Sowerby Ellison Glassworks, Gateshead
	March	27	13	Sowerby Ellison Glassworks, Gateshead
	March	28	7	Sowerby Ellison Glassworks, Gateshead
	April	28	2	John Derbyshire and Co., Manchester
	May	8	6	Sowerby Ellison Glassworks, Gateshead
	May	13	3	Charles Harris, Birmingham
	May	17	9	John Derbyshire and Co., Manchester
	May	24	5	Sowerby Ellison Glassworks, Gateshead
	May	29	19	Sowerby Ellison Glassworks, Gateshead
	June	6	2	Whittingham and Percival, Manchester
	June	14	2	Whittingham and Percival, Birmingham
	June	20	1	Sowerby Ellison Glassworks, Gateshead
	June	21	1	Sowerby Ellison Glassworks, Gateshead

Year	Month	Day	Bundle	Firm Registering the Design
	July	24	13	Sowerby Ellison Glassworks, Gateshead
	July	29	6	Henry Greener, Sunderland
	August	18	10	Sowerby Ellison Glassworks, Gateshead
	October	16	8	Sowerby Ellison Glassworks, Gateshead
	November	15	4	Sowerby Ellison Glassworks, Gateshead
	November	28	10	James Derbyshire and Sons, Manchester
	December	19	16	Andrew Ker, Manchester
1877	January	16	8	George Davidson and Co., Gateshead
	January	16	11	Sowerby Ellison Glassworks, Gateshead
	February	13	8	Sowerby Ellison Glassworks, Gateshead
	February	23	8	Sowerby Ellison Glassworks, Gateshead
	February	28	15	George Davidson and Co., Gateshead
	March	1	5	Sowerby Ellison Glassworks, Gateshead
	March	8	13	S. Maw, Son and Thompson, London
	March	13	10	Sowerby Ellison Glassworks, Gateshead
	March	15	1	Sowerby Ellison Glassworks, Gateshead
	March	19	15	Sowerby Ellison Glassworks, Gateshead
	March	21	4	Regent Flint Glass Co., Manchester
	March	22	12	Sowerby Ellison Glassworks, Gateshead
	March	23	7	Sowerby Ellison Glassworks, Gateshead

March	29	4	Sowerby Ellison Glassworks, Gateshead
May	4	4	Regent Flint Glass Co., Manchester
May	31	9	Sowerby Ellison Glassworks, Gateshead
September	4	3	James Henry Stone, Birmingham
September	18	7	Sowerby Ellison Glassworks, Gateshead
October	13	12	G. V. de Luca, London
October	17	2	Molineaux, Webb and Co., Manchester
October	29	2	Sowerby Ellison Glassworks, Gateshead
November	20	4	Sowerby Ellison Glassworks, Gateshead
December	3	2	Molineaux, Webb and Co., Manchester
December	6	3	Molineaux, Webb and Co., Manchester
December	17	12	Sowerby Ellison Glassworks, Gateshead
December	19	1	Sowerby Ellison Glassworks, Gateshead
1878 January	20	3	Sowerby Ellison Glassworks, Gateshead
March	1	8	Percival, Vickers and Co., Manchester
March	20	7	Sowerby Ellison Glassworks, Gateshead
March	22	8	Sowerby Ellison Glassworks, Gateshead
May	14	9	Sowerby Ellison Glassworks, Gateshead
June	8	11	Henry Greener, Sunderland
June	25	10	Sowerby Ellison Glassworks, Gateshead

Year	Month	Day	Bundle	Firms Registering the Design
	July	8	9	Sowerby Ellison Glassworks, Gateshead
	July	29	4	Sowerby Ellison Glassworks, Gateshead
	August	12	6	Sowerby Ellison Glassworks, Gateshead
	August	16	11	Sowerby Ellison Glassworks, Gateshead
	August	30	16	Sowerby Ellison Glassworks, Gateshead
	August	31	8	Henry Greener, Sunderland
	September	23	6	George Davidson and Co., Gateshead
	November	4	10	Sowerby Ellison Glassworks, Gateshead
	November	7	17	Sowerby Ellison Glassworks, Gateshead
	November	20	11	Sowerby Ellison Glassworks, Gateshead
	December	13	6	Sowerby Ellison Glassworks, Gateshead
	December	23	2	Sowerby Ellison Glassworks, Gateshead
1879	January	8	10	Sowerby Ellison Glassworks, Gateshead
	February	8	8	Sowerby Ellison Glassworks, Gateshead
	February	12	17	Sowerby Ellison Glassworks, Gateshead
	March	10	9	Sowerby Ellison Glassworks, Gateshead
	March	17	11	Sowerby Ellison Glassworks, Gateshead
	April	28	7	Sowerby Ellison Glassworks, Gateshead
	June	4	1	Rochester Tumbler Co., Pittsburgh, USA

June	6	10	Sowerby Ellison Glassworks, Gateshead
June	30	14	Sowerby Ellison Glassworks, Gateshead
July	3	6	John Shaw, Latimer Works, Sheffield
July	22	6	Sowerby Ellison Glassworks, Gateshead
July	29	13	Sowerby Ellison Glassworks, Gateshead
August	14	15	Sowerby Ellison Glassworks, Gateshead
September	4	7	Sowerby Ellison Glassworks, Gateshead
September	12	13	Sowerby Ellison Glassworks, Gateshead
September	18	13	Sowerby Ellison Glassworks, Gateshead
September	19	19	Henry Greener, Sunderland
September	23	2	Molineaux, Webb and Co., Manchester
September	23	13	Sowerby Ellison Glassworks, Gateshead
December	2	21	Sowerby Ellison Glassworks, Gateshead
1880 January	5	2	Molineaux, Webb and Co., Manchester
January	7	2	Molineaux, Webb and Co., Manchester
January	9	11	Sowerby Ellison Glassworks, Gateshead
January	14	2	Molineaux, Webb and Co., Manchester
February	4	13	Rochester Tumbler Co., Pittsburgh, USA
February	13	3	Rochester Tumbler Co., Pittsburgh, USA

Year	Month	Day	Bundle	Firm Registering the Design
	February	17	9	William Henry Heppell, Newcastle
	March	20	2	John Shaw, Latimer Works, Sheffield
	May	24	8	Sowerby Ellison Glassworks, Gateshead
	June	19	16	William Henry Heppell, Newcastle
	July	13	11	William Henry Heppell, Newcastle
	July	26	10	William Henry Heppell, Newcastle
	July	27	9	Percival, Vickers and Co., Manchester
	September	14	1	Sowerby Ellison Glassworks, Gateshead
	September	24	9	Sowerby Ellison Glassworks, Gateshead
	November	9	1	James Bird, Britannia Works, Bilston
	December	3	15	J. Defries and Sons, Houndsditch, London
	December	8	14	Henry Greener, Sunderland
	December	18	15	William Henry Heppell and Co., Newcastle
1881	February	8	4	John Shaw, Latimer Works, Sheffield
	March	1	8	Max Sugar, Holborn Circus, London
	March	11	2	Sowerby Ellison Glassworks, Gateshead
	March	19	11	Sowerby Ellison Glassworks, Gateshead
	April	4	6	William Pratt, Icknield Street, Birmingham
	April	20	9	Sowerby Ellison Glassworks, Gateshead
	April	21	13	Henry Greener, Sunderland

	May	19	9	Sowerby Ellison Glassworks, Gateshead
	June	14	9	Henry Greener, Sunderland
	June	24	10	Henry Greener, Sunderland
	September 21	16	Sowerby Ellison Glassworks, Gateshead
	September 26	1	William Henry Heppell, Newcastle
	September 28	3	Molineaux, Webb and Co., Manchester
	October	12	5	Molineaux, Webb and Co., Manchester
	October	22	15	Percival, Vickers Ltd, Manchester
	November	7	3	William Henry Heppell, Newcastle
	December	6	13	William Henry Heppell, Newcastle
	December	14	6	Sowerby Ellison Glassworks, Gateshead
	December	15	10	Sowerby Ellison Glassworks, Gateshead
1882	January	2	1	Molineaux, Webb and Co., Manchester
	February	9	20	Sowerby Ellison Glassworks, Gateshead
	March	17	4	Percival, Vickers Ltd, Manchester
	April	24	2	John Short Downing, Birmingham
	April	28	12	Sowerby Ellison Glassworks, Gateshead
	May	25	1	Percival, Vickers and Co., Manchester
	May	25	12	Henry Greener, Sunderland
	July	19	6	Henry Greener, Sunderland
	August	9	14	Sowerby Ellison Glassworks, Gateshead
	August	29	13	Sowerby Ellison Glassworks, Gateshead

Year	Month	Day	Bundle	Firm Registering the Design
	October	25	16	Sowerby Ellison Glassworks, Gateshead
	November	24	17	William Henry Heppell, Newcastle
	November	27	1	Percival, Vickers and Co., Manchester
1883	February	3	11	Sowerby Ellison Glassworks, Gateshead
	February	12	9	William Henry Heppell, Newcastle
	February	14	11	Percival, Vickers and Co., Manchester
	March	27	5	Boulton and Mills, Stourbridge
	April	17	3	Percival, Vickers and Co., Manchester
	August	24	2	Percival, Vickers and Co., Manchester
	November	2	12	Percival, Vickers and Co., Manchester

From 1 January 1884 a new method of identifying registered designs was introduced. The previous thirteen groups were abandoned and a single numerical list was used for all objects. Since designs were registered at the rate of something over 20,000 per year it would be a formidable task to isolate those numbers relating to pressed-glass items. However, in order to assist in dating the first year of a design, the following list gives the number of the initial design registered on 1 January each year, up to 1901.

1884	1	1893	205240
1885	19754	1894	224720
1886	40480	1895	246975
1887	64520	1896	268392
1888	90483	1897	291241
1889	116648	1898	311658
1890	141273	1899	331707
1891	163767	1900	351202
1892	185713	1901	368154

LIST OF GLASS PATENTS

The following is a list of glass patents registered by the major glasshouses in the north-east of England – Sowerby, Davidson and Greener – between 1870 and 1900. Further details can be obtained from the library of the Patent Office, 25 Southampton Buildings, Chancery Lane, High Holborn, London WC2.

J. G. Sowerby, Gateshead

Patent No.	Date	Description
2433	15 September 1871	Ornamenting pressed glass
4065	1874	Presses for moulding glass
2156	29 May 1878	Making glass of a novel colour effect
522	6 February 1880	Producing stained glass
1449	8 April 1880	Graduated glass for medical use
4505	15 October 1881	Pressed glass
697	8 February 1883	Tools for etching on glass
758	12 February 1883	Pressing glass
6463	27 May 1885	Moulds for glassware
6739	3 June 1885	Moulding articles of glass
6937	8 June 1885	Moulding articles of glass
4509	31 March 1886	Fire-polishing glass
6150	6 May 1886	Fire-polishing glass
12001	5 September 1887	Polishing cut glass
7400	1889	Making glass funnels
17565	1889	Antique and sheet glass
20619	1889	Cutting glass cylinders
3286	1 March 1890	Glass
7826	6 May 1891	Glass bottles
1943	1 February 1892	Treating glass

3056	11 February 1896	Fire-polishing glass
19664	5 September 1896	Glass globes and shades

J. G. Davidson, Gateshead

3424	25 August 1879	Finishing pressed or moulded glass tumblers
2641	1889	Articles of pressed glass
8049	1889	Pressed glass dishes
8531	1889	Shades for gas burners
20394	13 December 1890	Pressed glass dishes, etc.
11906	25 June 1892	Glass dishes and baskets
624	9 January 1897	Ship's signal lamps
16896	22 September 1900	Flushing cisterns
7830	31 March 1910	Glass flower blocks, etc.

Henry Greener, Sunderland

3025	15 September 1873	Decanters and jugs
268	1874	Glass letters and figures
4531	30 November 1877	Glasses for carriage roof lamps

GLOSSARY

annealing: The process whereby newly formed glass objects are cooled slowly, over many hours, from their high working temperature in order to prevent stresses and strains developing in the material.

batch: The term applied to the mixture of raw materials which when heated together fuse to form glass.

blow iron: A long hollow metal tube used in *free-blown* and *blow-moulded* glass manufacture to collect the initial *gather* of molten *metal* which is then blown into a balloon before being further worked.

blow-moulded: Glass objects produced by the molten *metal* on the end of a *blow iron* being blown up inside a multi-part metal *mould* which imparts shape and design to the outer surface of the glass.

chair: A dual term applied either to the traditional wooden seat with long flat arms used by the craftsman when working the glass or to the team of men who work in the production of glass articles.

charcoal: Amorphous carbon used as a colouring agent. In small quantities it produces a yellow colour in *soda glass*; in larger quantities it produces opaque black.

cobalt: Used as the oxide, is a powerful colouring agent. A small quantity produces a deep blue colour, whilst increasing the amount produces a glass which is black by reflected light and a very deep blue by transmitted light.

collar: In glass pressing, a term applied to the metal ring at the top of the *mould* which prevents the glass being pressed out of the mould and also shapes the upper rim of the article.

commemorative glass: Glass bearing inscriptions, designs or portraits relating to people, places and things commemorating events of importance or interest.

copper: Used as the oxide, is a colouring agent which produces a blue, green or ruby colour depending on the chemical conditions present during melting. Can also be used as bright metal flakes which remain unchanged in the glass, so-called aventurine.

cullet: Refers to broken glass of all descriptions either accumulated as waste during manufacture or from rejects. It is a valuable source of glassmaking material, and a certain amount, suitably selected and cleaned, is used as a *batch* ingredient.

decolouriser: A chemical, usually manganese or arsenic, which is added to glass, in small quantities, to neutralise the natural greenish colour caused by the presence of iron. Iron in glass absorbs light rays at the red end of the spectrum, allowing the yellow and blue rays to be transmitted and appear as green. Manganese, on the other hand, absorbs the blue and yellow rays leaving the red to be transmitted, thus producing a balance of light rays which then appear as white, although in diminished quantity. If large amounts of manganese and iron are present, so much light is absorbed that none is transmitted and the glass appears as opaque black.

engraving: Designs produced on glass by cutting into its surface either with a diamond point or a small rotating copper disc charged with an abrasive material.

etching: Design produced on glass by the use of hydrofluoric acid which dissolves glass. The technique is known as 'wax resist' in which the surface of the glass is protected by a coat of wax which resists the action of the acid. The parts of the design to be eaten into the glass are cut away giving the acid access to the glass surface.

fire-polishing: The process of reheating the newly pressed article at the mouth of the furnace or in a *glory hole*, which almost melts the surface and produces a smooth finish. It also helps to remove '*fins*' and *mould lines*.

fins: Thin protrusions of glass which appear along *mould lines* and are caused by the molten glass being forced into the spaces between the various parts of the mould (see Plate 5).

flint glass: Usually used to describe a heavy glass containing lead oxide but often used indiscriminately to describe colourless as opposed to coloured glass.

free-blown: Glass blown into a balloon and then worked into shape using simple tools without the use of *moulds*.

gaffer: The craftsman, heading a small team of workmen, who undertakes the skilled finishing work in *free-blown* and *blow-moulded* glass.

gather: A quantity of glass taken up from a furnace *pot* on the end of a *blow iron* or *pontil rod*.

gatherer: The member of the pressing team who collects the *gather* and then brings it to the press.

Glass Excise Tax: A tax levied on the raw materials of glass manufacture, by weight, between 1745 and 1845.

glory hole: A small opening either in the main furnace or elsewhere giving access to a heat source where articles can be *fire-polished*.

gold: Used as a colouring agent, in the form of certain salts, to produce a deep red colour.

iron: Generally found as an impurity in glassmaking materials but is also used intentionally as the oxide to give a deep green colour. Mixed in the correct proportions with manganese oxide, it gives a deep brown colour.

lead glass: A high-quality heavy glass, also called *flint glass*, used in the manufacture of early pressed glass and in all good quality *free-blown* and *blow-moulded* glass. The main constituents are silica and lead oxide.

lehr: A long tunnel oven with a heat gradient along which newly made glass is transported during *annealing*. At its entry the temperature is near to red heat and its exit is at room temperature.

manganese: Used as a decolouriser, or colouring agent as the oxide. It gives a beautiful amethyst colour.

melter: The member of the pressing team who receives the article from the *mould* and *fire-polishes* it.

metal: In the glass trade, another name for glass either in the molten or finished state.

metallic oxides: These are the colouring agents of glass. They can be used to produce more than one colour depending on the chemical conditions to which they are submitted during melting, e.g. an oxidising or a reducing atmosphere.

mould: In pressed glass the receptacle into which the molten glass is pressed to give it form and impress a design on its surface. Usually the outer mould is made up of a number of parts hinged together. The inner mould which forms the plunger and transmits the pressure may also carry a design.

mould lines: The raised lines left on pressed glass by contact with the joints in the *mould*. They can be diminished by *fire-polishing*.

nickel: Used as a colouring agent, may give two colours depending on conditions. Used in glass containing potash, it gives a deep violet colour, whilst in soda-lime glass it produces yellow.

opaline: An opalescent glass produced by the addition of cryolite or arsenic to the *batch*. Appears milky by reflected light and shows many blue and golden tints by transmitted light.

pontil or punty rod: A solid rod of iron used for collecting a *gather* of glass for pressing or for attaching to a pressed object prior to *fire-polishing*. After 1860 those used for fire-polishing were fitted with a *spring clip* to hold the objects.

pontil or punty mark: The mark left behind on the base of a glass object after the *pontil rod* has been removed. Found on some early pressed glass before 1860, particularly goblets and tumblers. Usually left rough on pressed goods but occasionally ground smooth as on better-quality glass.

pot: The hooded vessel made of fireclay, inserted into the furnace and used to hold the *batch* during melting and fusion.

presser: The member of the pressing team who actually pulls the lever and presses the article.

soda glass: A soft light glass used in pressing, cheaper than *lead glass*. Its chief constituents are silica and sodium carbonate or soda ash which is a good flux and lowers the temperature at which the glass will melt.

spooner: A small stubby vase used in the second half of the nineteenth century for holding teaspoons.

spring clip: A three-pronged holder attached to the end of a *pontil rod* for holding objects during *fire-polishing*. Sowerby's patented the idea of fitting them with asbestos pads in the 1880s.

BIBLIOGRAPHY

Belknap, E. M.: *Milk Glass*. Crown Publishers, New York, 1949.

Butterworth, L. M. Angus: *British Table and Ornamental Glass*. Leonard Hill, 1956.

Chance, Henry: *Principles of Glassmaking*. London, 1883.

Davis, D., and Middlemas, K.: *Coloured Glass*. Herbert Jenkins, 1968.

Elville, E. M.: *Collector's Dictionary of Glass*. Country Life, 1961.

Glass Research Association Bulletin, 1922–4.

Godden, Geoffrey A.: *Antique Glass and China under £5*. Arthur Barker, 1966.

Lattimore, C. R.: 'English Decorative Press Moulded Glass', in *Antique Dealer and Collector's Guide*, February 1978.

McKearin, G. S. and H.: *American Glass*. Crown Publishers, New York, 1941.

Parsons, Charles: *Patents, Designs and Trade Marks*. Technical Press, 1938.

Pellatt, Apsley: *Curiosities of Glass Making*. London, 1849.

Pottery Gazette and Glass Trades Review, 1874–1900.

Revi, Albert C.: *Nineteenth-Century Glass*. Thomas Nelson & Sons, New York, 1959.

The Glass Review, Dept of Technology, University of Sheffield, 1927–30.

Thorpe, W. A.: *English Glass*. 1st edn, A. & C. Black, 1935.

Wakefield, Hugh: *Nineteenth Century British Glass*. Faber and Faber, 1961.

Webber, Norman W.: *Collecting Glass*, David and Charles, 1972.

INDEX